Initiation to
Chaldean
Numerology

Unveils the Secret Power of the Numbers

with The Tables and Calculations
for Your Inner Guidance

TEMPLUM DİANAE

- MEDİA -

contents included

Congratulations on getting this book!
If you want to attract and manifest more Love and Abundance
and discover more about spirituality, join the Templum Dianae
community and get 1 MP3 of guided meditation to awaken your
inner self.

This guided meditation is designed to manifest tui desires in
daily life!

Follow this link
templumdianae.com/en/bookmp3/

İF YOU DO NOT KNOW TEMPLUM DİANAE

Do you feel lost, disconnected from your deepest essence?

You have tried everything: meditation, yoga, spiritual readings. Yet, that inner emptiness persists. Relationships don't take off, money seems to elude you, and serenity is a distant mirage.

It is time to stop circling the problem and face it head-on.

Welcome to *Templum Dianae*, the place where women awaken to their authentic power. Born in Italy in 2013, our blog is written **by witches for witches**. We do not hide behind sweet words or vain promises. We are here to shake you up, provoke you, push you beyond your limits.

Why settle for a mediocre life when you can have everything you want?

Every month, more than **247,000 people** come into contact with our materials through all our channels. *Templum Dianae Media* is the beating heart of this movement, a publishing project that publishes hundreds of books each year in over **6 languages**. From revolutionary new texts to republications of ancient grimoires, we offer powerful tools to transform your reality.

It is not just theory. It is practice, action, transformation.

Here's what some women who have changed their lives because of us say:

"Thanks to Templum Dianae, I attracted authentic love into my life. Toxic relationships are a thing of the past." - **Sara M.**

"Economic manifestation techniques really work. I have seen my bank account grow like never before." - **Luisa D.**

"I found myself again. The connection with my inner power became unbreakable." - **Elena F.**

Are you ready to stop surviving and start really living?

This book is not for the faint of heart. It is for those who are ready to look in the mirror unfiltered, embrace their shadow and turn it into light.

Don't waste any more time. Every page you read will be a step toward the powerful woman you are meant to be.

The journey begins now. Are you with us?

İNDEX

Contents

İNİTİATİON TO NUMEROLOGY

Welcome, Seeker.

Have you already felt that subtle tremor creeping through your thoughts? It is the call of the unknown, of the mystery that hovers above every figure, every symbol that your soul has always longed to decipher.

How is Your Path progressing?

Perhaps you feel it fraught with obstacles, or perhaps a little lost, searching for direction. This is normal, especially when you are approaching ancient knowledge such as Chaldean Numerology, which for centuries concealed its secrets from those who were not ready.

In the months leading up to this moment, I have written countless words, filled pages and pages of forgotten wisdom, trying to bring out the depth of this sacred art. Yet, many have confessed to feeling overwhelmed, lost among the numbers, unable to grasp the true message behind the mathematics of the soul. And here, failure is often attributed to the student, as if it were his or her fault for not understanding.

But listen to me well. You are not wrong. You have never been wrong.

The problem is that too many people, posing as spiritual guides, actually do nothing but fuel confusion. They have built a whole market around your need for answers, and they sell you false promises. They hide behind words like "circle," "forest," pretending to welcome you, but often what you get are invisible chains, ready to clutch your soul and distort your purity for ends that do not belong to you. This is not my path, and it will not be yours.

I am here to really guide you, with humility and respect for your research. That is why I have chosen to review every concept, to distill the ancient knowledge of Chaldean numerology and offer it to you in a clear, accessible way, without ever diminishing its depth. Because you deserve to understand. You deserve to see the design hidden in the folds of your destiny.

This is just the beginning, a first step on a journey that will lead you to rewrite the paradigms that have accompanied you so far. You will learn to recognize the signs, the numbers that speak to your soul, and discover how to apply this wisdom to your life, your heart, your path.

Are you ready to find out what the numbers say about you?

Chaldean numerology

Although numerology is spoken of in many forms today, there is one system that, in the silence of the centuries, has stood out for its almost uncanny precision: **Chaldean Numerology**. An ancient, mysterious system that has proven its power and truth to me whenever I have dared to listen to it.

The Chaldeans, wise observers of energy, were the first to understand a profound principle: **everything is vibration.** Every sound, every number, every letter carries an energy that moves through you and the world, influencing your path, your choices, your innermost feelings. They have connected sounds to vibrations, vibrations to numbers, and numbers to letters, creating a secret language that you are now about to learn to decipher.

Unlike other systems, Chaldean Numerology does not just look superficially at your name or date of birth. **It digs deeper**. Every single letter of your name hides a vibration, a meaning that speaks of you, your unique energy. And it doesn't stop there. Your life path, what you came here to do, be or learn, is revealed through the vibrations of the numbers that accompany you from your very first breath.

This system, while long forgotten, is not as difficult as they say. Yes, its ancient complexity might seem intimidating, but once you unlock its secrets, it will become a valuable ally, a beacon in the darkness of your doubts and uncertainties.

It will give you a map not only of yourself, but also of the people you cross on your path.

Imagine having a personal blueprint to guide you in every decision. A way to understand why certain relationships come into your life and others leave, why some paths seem impassable to you while others attract you like magnets.

 Chaldean Numerology not only offers you this understanding, but also enables you to see beyond the visible, to sense the energies around you and use them to illuminate your sentimental and spiritual path.

The ancient Chaldeans

More than two thousand years ago, in a place kissed by the Tigris and Euphrates rivers, lay a land shrouded in mystery: ancient Chaldea. This people, whose true origins are still little known today, occupied the southern part of Babylon, a cradle of wisdom and power. The Chaldeans ascended the throne of Babylon and for more than seventy-five years, under kings such as Nebuchadnezzar, shaped the destiny of one of the most fascinating civilizations in history.

But they were not just conquerors. They were visionaries.

To a world already rich in agriculture and manufacturing, **the Chaldeans brought something more**: deep knowledge, an understanding of the universe that transcended the visible. By introducing astrology, sacred mathematics and advanced spiritual rituals, they laid the foundation for a society that worshipped the stars and the mysteries hidden in their glow. Moon worship, magic, divination--these were tools they used to decipher the subtle energies that permeated reality.

It is no accident that Babylon is often remembered as the "cradle of civilization." Yet what makes this people even more intriguing is the fact that **few written traces** remain of them. Most of what we know about the Chaldeans comes not from them themselves, but from the civilizations that followed them.

And it is precisely this aura of mystery that makes their spiritual legacy all the more fascinating.

Of all their knowledge, one has survived intact, crossing the millennia: **Chaldean Numerology**.

An ancient system that measures energies so accurately that it seems almost magical. This method does not just draw lines and numbers; it is a secret code that invites you to look beyond the visible, to discover the vibrations that govern your life. Every number, every letter carries with it a deep meaning, a resonance that speaks to you in the silent language of the universe.

Try listening to it.

Experience the power of this system on yourself and let it amaze you.

Its roots are in the oldest wisdom, but its fruits can illuminate your life today, offering guidance in understanding who you really are, what you desire, and how you can improve your emotional and spiritual situation.

The history of numerology

When you approach numerology, it is easy to get lost in historical details, trying to understand which civilizations contributed to the development of this mysterious field. But, if you allow, let me guide you to a deeper vision that goes beyond time and space.

Numerology is not just a man-made system. No, it is something more. **It is a universal code**, an invisible structure that governs everything that exists, from the movement of the stars to the most intimate emotions you feel in your heart. Mathematics, in its purest form, is not an invention but a discovery. It is as if numbers have always existed, hidden in the shadows, ready to reveal their secrets to anyone who knows how to listen.

The ancients understood this. Not only the Egyptians or the peoples of Mesopotamia, of whom we have more or less obvious traces today. Even more remote civilizations, of which we know barely a few fragments, sensed that numbers were a key to understanding **the energies that govern the world and the human soul**.

Have you ever thought that there is knowledge that has been lost over time?

Spiritual technologies, advanced wisdom systems that enabled the ancients to communicate with cosmic forces in ways we can only imagine today. Perhaps, in those distant ages, numbers were not just tools for counting, but were true **channels of connection with the universe**, capable of revealing the most hidden truths.

Chaldean Numerology is one such system, one of the few that has managed to survive the passage of millennia. But even this ancient knowledge is not just a legacy of a single culture. **It is a window into something much larger**. A fragment of a universal truth that resonates through the ages, bringing you a message of power and transformation.

When you look at the numbers around you, don't just think of one civilization or culture. **Think about the whole universe**. About those invisible forces that intertwine your desires, your emotions, and your destiny. Every number, every vibration has a role, a meaning, and every time you tune into them, you discover a new piece of the puzzle of your life.

Open your heart and mind to this possibility: let the numbers not be mere symbols, but **lead them toward knowing yourself and your path**.

 Do not limit yourself to what is written in the ancient texts. Imagine that there is much more to be discovered, a forgotten knowledge that is waiting for you to be unearthed.

The Ancients and the Discovery of Numerology

Your journey into numerology begins from a deep and ancient place, where nature itself whispers secrets just waiting to be discovered. The story of this knowledge is not simply a set of numbers, but a **revelation of the spiritual forces** that permeate every corner of the world. The ancients, with their intimate and respectful connection to the earth, were the first to sense that what is visible holds something much greater.

Through daily observation of the natural world, they began to notice that some elements-such as crystals, herbs, even rocks-were not just physical objects, but carriers of **subtle energies and spiritual powers**. Everything in nature possessed a hidden meaning, a secret order that the ancients recognized and honored. **It was this insight that guided them** to a deeper understanding of the laws governing the universe, both the visible and invisible.

Every crystal they touched, every herb they picked, was not just a material resource, but a **mirror of the spiritual forces** permeating reality. The vibrations of these natural elements were linked to particular spiritual properties, creating an invisible map of the energy flowing through the world. This subtle but powerful awareness was the first step toward creating a system of knowledge that embraced both the visible and the invisible.

But the real leap occurred when the ancients lifted their eyes to the heavens.

The stars, the moon, the sun-they were not mere celestial bodies. **They were manifestations of divine forces**, carriers of messages and influences that shaped every aspect of life on Earth. The ancients knew that understanding the cycles of the heavens also meant understanding their own destiny. Every movement of the stars reflected a cosmic order, a sacred dance that influenced the tides, crops and even the beating of the human heart.

From these observations arose the need to create a system that could codify this connection between heaven and earth. And thus were born the laws of numerology. **Numbers** were not just symbols or tools for counting, but expressions of divine principles. Through them, it was possible to map and interpret the cosmic and spiritual forces that govern reality. **Each number was a bridge** between what is earthly and what is heavenly, between the material and the spiritual.

In this context, the Greek myth of Uranus takes on new meaning. Uranus, the sky god, was not only a lord of celestial phenomena, but also the father of all occult sciences, including astrology and numerology. His clash with Cronus, the god of time, represents not only a conflict, but the **creation of new knowledge** and cosmic forces that influence the human world. Uranus, with its celestial wisdom, symbolizes the origin of astrological and numerological wisdom, making its study essential for those who, like you, want to understand the hidden laws that govern their destiny.

Numerology, then, is not just a study of numbers, but a deep journey **into the forces that move the world and the soul**. A journey that will lead you to discover your role in this vast and mysterious universe, and to understand how invisible energies influence your life, your relationships and your path.

The Fall of Atlantis and the Dispersion of the Ancient Sciences.

The legend of Atlantis is not just about a physical catastrophe. It is the tale of a profound loss, an open wound in the heart of human knowledge. Atlantis, according to the myth, was not only an extraordinary civilization for its technologies, but **a beacon of spiritual wisdom**, a place where understanding of cosmic and divine laws far exceeded that of other civilizations. Their fall marked not only the destruction of an island, but the dispersal of knowledge accumulated over millennia, knowledge that touched the deepest chords of reality.

When Atlantis sank to the depths, its knowledge was not lost entirely. The ancient Atlanteans, driven by the need to survive, fled to distant lands, taking with them fragments of what they had discovered. **Advanced practices of numerology, astrology and esoteric knowledge** traveled with them, crossing continents and cultures, leaving subtle but significant traces in the hearts of surviving civilizations.

But time, like a slow tide, erodes everything it touches. And so, those sacred sciences, devoutly guarded, began to fragment.

Many of these practices were reduced to superstitions, lost their original meaning, while sacred symbols and numbers were misunderstood or trivialized. What was once a deep connection with the universe became a series of empty rituals, a distorted memory of an ancient science now forgotten.

Despite this, the fragments of Atlantis did not disappear completely. Today, there is an awakening. **Scholars, esotericists and spiritualists** are trying to reconstruct what was lost, delving into the myths, ancient texts, and symbols that still echo in our collective subconscious. There is a growing desire to reconnect with that ancient wisdom, to bring to light those forgotten truths that somehow can still illuminate the present.

Atlantis represents not only a tragic past, but a **grazed possibility**, a society that lived in harmony with cosmic and spiritual laws, that understood the subtle interweaving of the soul and the universe.

Rediscovering their lost science, integrating that knowledge into our world, could **reconnect us with a lost balance**, a worldview in which the material and the spiritual walk together, aligned with the natural forces that govern us.

Numbers as keys to time

The ancients did not see time as a mere succession of hours or days. To them, time was something broader, a fabric interwoven with space, energy and spirituality. **Through numerology**, they believed they had discovered a key to interact with these dimensions, using numbers not only to understand reality but to shape it. With complex patterns and careful calculations, they sought to influence events, direct cosmic energies, and even alter the perception of time itself.

This knowledge, however mysterious and ancient, has not been completely lost. According to many esoteric traditions, the ancient masters of numerology, including those from legendary Atlantis, continue to communicate through the centuries, sending messages in the form of **recurring numerical sequences**. These are signs, indications of a knowledge that has never quite died out. Many practitioners of contemporary mysticism say they perceive these sequences as real codes that guide their spiritual path, suggesting directions, answers and solutions.

The legacy of the Atlanteans, as well as other vanished civilizations, has never been entirely forgotten. On the contrary, today we are rediscovering and integrating that knowledge that once seemed unattainable. As our understanding of the esoteric sciences evolves, we are getting closer to that point where numerology was a sacred science, capable of guiding our personal and spiritual development.

This **rediscovery is not just an archaeological search for lost knowledge**; it is an evolutionary leap in our awareness. Using numerological keys, we are learning to reconnect with the forces around us, to manipulate those subtle links between time and space, and to influence the energies that guide our daily existence. Numbers become not only tools for understanding our reality, but **doors to a new understanding of the universe**.

What the ancients have left us are not just enigmatic symbols or traces of a glorious past. They have given us a sophisticated system of numerological knowledge, a language with which we can converse with the universe. **Every number we decode**, every sequence we understand, brings us closer to that forgotten knowledge, opening paths that lead us to explore new levels of personal and collective growth.

Numerology, as it was understood by the ancients, is not just a practice of calculation. **It is a key to understanding universal dynamics**, a bridge between the visible and the invisible, between what is earthly and what is divine.

THE ORİGİNS OF CHALDEAN NUMERALS

In the previous chapter, you got your first glimpse of the history of the Chaldeans and the roots of numerology. Now, it's time to dive deeper into the origins of **Chaldean Numerology**, exploring those associations that give it life and meaning. It is essential to understand these connections before you start making calculations, because without a clear understanding of the underlying energies, Chaldean Numerology can seem complex, and many end up getting lost in its intricate secrets.

The Chaldeans knew that every number and letter were more than just symbols. They were manifestations of subtle energies, invisible threads connecting every aspect of existence. Numbers were not mere counting tools; they were the very language of the universe, charged with spiritual vibrations. That is why understanding the deeper meaning of these associations is the first step in decoding their power.

Chaldean Numerology does not follow the rules of more modern numerology, which simply links a number to a letter based on the alphabet. This ancient system is different, more nuanced and mysterious. Each letter and number carries with it a resonance, a unique vibration that interacts with the others in complex ways, often invisible to the untrained eye. **Understanding these connections allows you to align with**

cosmic forces, to see the hidden pattern that governs your choices, your encounters, and your relationships.

But without this understanding, the Chaldean system can seem impenetrable. **Many people fail in Chaldean Numerology precisely because they try to use it as if it were a simple mathematical calculation.** They try to reduce it to numbers without grasping the deep vibrations, the energies these numbers carry. They are confronted with a wall of symbols that they cannot decipher, getting lost in numbers and formulas without grasping the spiritual essence that animates them.

Chaldean Numerology is an art that requires time, patience and deep listening. Every number, every letter carries a fragment of your destiny, but to see clearly, you must first prepare yourself to understand these hidden connections. Only then will the numerological calculations begin to speak to you, revealing the truths that have always been there, waiting to be discovered.

This awareness is the true beginning of your journey in Chaldean Numerology

The numbers of Chaldean tablets

Chaldean tablets, an incredible collection of ancient clay artifacts, are a valuable window into the life and beliefs of a civilization that left an indelible mark throughout history. These artifacts, more than just archaeological objects, tell us about a people-the Chaldeans-who, in the fertile land of Mesopotamia, intertwined their destiny with that of the stars and cosmic energies.

Their discovery dates back to the 19th century, when archaeologists began excavating the ruins of ancient cities such as Babylon and Ur. These tablets, which remained buried for millennia, **bear imprinted traces of ancient** knowledge, knowledge that the Chaldeans carefully codified. Made of fresh clay and engraved with cuneiform writing while the material was still soft, they were then baked in the sun or in kilns to make them immortal in time.

 It is as if those symbols wanted to speak across the border of centuries, preserving intact the secrets of a civilization that communicated not only with its words, but with the entire universe.

Cuneiform writing, traced with a stylus on these tablets, was a complex language of wedge-shaped signs that revealed much more than what appears at first glance. The engraved texts cover a wide range of topics, ranging from legal decrees and trade records to personal correspondence, but it is the mathematical and astronomical knowledge that emerges from these tablets that reveals the most fascinating aspect of Chaldean culture.

The Chaldeans **were masters of astronomy and mathematics**, and these tablets document their observations of the heavens and the calculations that guided them. They did not simply observe the stars, but revered them as keys to decipher cosmic laws.

It was from these observations that the earliest forms of astrology and understanding of lunar cycles were born, elements that were fundamental not only to their calendar but also to their spiritual practices.

Behind each sign etched into the clay lies a deep connection between the earthly and the divine. **These tablets** tell us of a civilization that knew how to interweave time and space, a people who looked to the stars not only to measure the passing of the seasons, but to understand their place in the universe.

Chaldean planetary numbers

Chaldean **tablets** hold an ancient and complex numerological system, intimately intertwined with astrology, reflecting the deep connection the Chaldeans perceived between **celestial bodies and numerical values**. This was not a simple numbers game, but a sacred system that revealed the secrets of destiny and human nature through planetary movements. Each planet, each number, was a fragment of a grand cosmic design, influencing not only daily events but the very essence of the soul.

The Chaldeans carefully observed the sky, accurately recording the trajectories of the planets and the phases of the moon, and in their clay tablets they engraved knowledge that transcended time. Each planet was associated with a number, and this connection was not accidental: it was the result of centuries of spiritual and astronomical observations. **Planets were seen as divine entities** that profoundly influenced human character and the course of events. These influences were measured through the language of numbers, which the Chaldeans used to decipher cosmic energies and their interactions with life on Earth.

In the **Chaldean Numerology** system, each number has a unique vibration, and these vibrations are directly related to particular planets. These were not simply numerical associations, but a deep harmonization between the universe and the individual. Numbers were tools for understanding the unseen forces that governed each person's destiny and character. **Each number resonated with a planetary energy**, which influenced the personality, talents and challenges a person would face throughout his or her life.

These associations were not only intellectual, but rooted in a more subtle and deeper perception of the spiritual qualities of numbers and planets. **The Chaldeans saw numbers as a key to attunement to the cosmic order**, to understanding the rhythms of the universe and one's place within it.

Through this numerological-planetary system, the Chaldeans believed they could not only understand their own destiny but also influence it by aligning themselves with the cosmic forces that governed the universe. **Numbers became bridges between the physical and spiritual worlds**, revealing the mysteries of life, death and human relationships. Their ability to associate numbers with planetary energies, and to do so with a precision that still amazes scholars today, shows how advanced their knowledge was.

Chaldean numerology was not only a tool for predicting the future, but a means of understanding the **flow of energy through the universe**. This knowledge, which has been preserved in clay tablets, continues to offer profound insights into the link between planets and numbers, revealing how celestial forces influence human life in subtle but powerful ways.

Chaldean astrology

Chaldean astrology is one of the oldest and most influential pillars of astrological wisdom, the roots of which go back to the mystical land of Babylon. The Chaldeans, inhabitants of Mesopotamia, observed the heavens as if they were an open book, reading the movements of the planets and stars not only to decipher the mysteries of the cosmos, but to **understand the divine plan** that governed every aspect of life, from the fate of empires to individual destiny.

Unlike modern astrology, which is based primarily on the seasons and uses the tropical zodiac, Chaldean astrology was **deeply connected with the stars**. It closely resembled sidereal astrology, which is still used today to plot the actual positions of constellations. The Chaldeans divided the sky into segments, each linked to a specific deity, with planets acting as intermediaries of their divine wills. Each planet had a name and a sacred role, influencing earthly life with uncanny precision.

Each planet represented a god and brought with it unique influences. **Jupiter** was associated with **Marduk**, the god of justice and royalty, a symbol of righteousness and authority. **Venus**, connected to **Ishtar**, represented not only love and fertility, but also war and burning passion that could turn into conflict. **Saturn**, connected **to Ninurta**, was the planet of agriculture and war, determining times of great prosperity or extreme hardship. The Chaldeans not only contemplated the sky, but minutely noted celestial events such as **eclipses**, planetary conjunctions, and heliacal risings (when a planet or star first appears at dawn). These events were seen as **divine omens**, signs that could herald radical changes, natural disasters, or political upheavals. A simple lunar eclipse, for example, could indicate the instability of a kingdom or the faltering health of a king, and such predictions influenced crucial political and social decisions.

Chaldean priests held extraordinary power, interpreting the heavens as a secret language of the gods. It was not uncommon for a king to rely on astrologers to make strategic decisions, from planning a battle to the ideal time to start planting. This **astrological priesthood** was not just symbolic: it held real influence over the fate of empires, guiding the choices of rulers with their star readings. There is also evidence that the Chaldeans practiced a primitive form of **natal astrology**, calculating the positions of the planets at the time of a person's birth to predict his or her character and destiny. This practice demonstrates an advanced understanding of the relationship between the individual and the cosmos, recognizing that each of us is part of a larger **cosmic order**, influenced by the same forces that move the stars.

Chaldean astrology was not only a sacred science, but a practical guide that governed daily life and political strategies. Their predictions served not only to peer into the future, but also to **harmonize human actions with the divine rhythm of the universe**. Rulers consulted the stars to plan wars, enact laws and even decide when to cultivate fields, showing how deeply rooted these beliefs were.

Even after the fall of Babylon, the legacy of Chaldean astrology did not die out. Its knowledge was absorbed and transformed by Greek and Indian astrological traditions, leaving a lasting imprint that still echoes in many esoteric practices today. The influence of this ancient system continues to shine, guiding generations through the centuries with its **cosmic wisdom**.

The planets according to the Chaldeans

To the Chaldeans, **each planet was more than just a celestial body**. Each star represented a deity, a sacred entity whose power and influence extended over all human life, from personal destiny to the fate of entire empires. **The movements of the planets** were not just astronomical phenomena, but true manifestations of divine will, signs that revealed the messages of the gods and the direction of cosmic energies.

Marduk and Jupiter

Marduk, the supreme deity of the Chaldean pantheon and patron of Babylon, was closely related to **Jupiter**, the largest and brightest of the planets visible to the naked eye. As **king of the gods**, Marduk represented cosmic order, justice and kingship. His power was perceived as crucial to maintaining balance in the world, and his influence was reflected in Jupiter's majestic movements in the night sky.

When **Jupiter** appeared, the Chaldeans saw it as a sign of stability and protection. **Jupiter's appearance** indicated Marduk's benevolent intervention, bringing order to cosmic chaos and reassuring kings about their reign. **His movements were carefully observed**, as they represented omens for the well-being of the ruler and the state, influencing not only politics but also the perception of the nation's future.

Jupiter was thus a tangible manifestation of Marduk's divine authority, a symbol of power and protection that resonated through the heavens, reminding everyone that the fate of kings and empires was written among the stars.

Ishtar and Venus

Ishtar, the powerful goddess of love and war, found her celestial reflection in **Venus**, the planet known for its extraordinary radiance and beauty. Like Ishtar, Venus embodied a dual nature: on the one hand she represented love, passion and fertility, and on the other the ferocity and destructive power of war. This contrast was reflected in the cycle of **Venus** as **morning star** and **evening star**, a transition that symbolized transformations in human life, as well as in nature.

Ishtar was invoked to influence both the most intimate feelings and the most violent battles, and Venus, with its celestial cycles, marked turning points in these areas. **Venus' transition** from morning star to evening star was an event of great astrological importance to the Chaldeans. When Venus rose as a **morning star**, it brought promises of new beginnings, blossoming passions and impending victories. As **an evening star**, on the other hand, it symbolized reflection, the closing of cycles and the power of inner transformation.

This double aspect of Ishtar-Venus represented **the complexity of human life**, where love and war were intertwined, and changes, marked by celestial cycles, influenced the dynamics of personal relationships and the fate of conflicts.

Ninurta and Saturn

Ninurta, the god of agriculture and war, was associated with **Saturn**, the darkest and most distant planet, whose slow path across the sky symbolized the inexorable power of time and fate. Ninurta, known for both his role as protector of crops and his destructive force in battle, embodied a balance between creation and destruction, growth and decline.

Saturn's slow orbit around the Sun perfectly reflected this nature. Like Ninurta, **Saturn** carried with him an ambivalent energy: he could be the harbinger of justice, bringing balance and abundance, but also of **deliberate destruction**, when it was necessary to tear down what was no longer fertile or just. Saturn's appearance in the sky was a signal that the Chaldeans watched carefully, as it could herald **times of great difficulty or abundance**.

In its agricultural dimension, Ninurta and Saturn influenced **crop planning**, indicating periods of prosperity or famine. In war, Saturn's presence marked the need to prepare with patience and determination, both to face impending conflicts and to withstand natural difficulties, such as disasters or adverse weather events. **Saturn** was thus a symbol of **strength and endurance**, but also of inevitable change, a silent guide for those who knew how to listen to its slow and powerful movements.

Nabu and Mercury

Nabu, the god of wisdom, writing and communication, found his celestial reflection in **Mercury**, the planet known for its rapid movements across the sky. The speed with which **Mercury** appeared and disappeared from the horizon perfectly reflected Nabu's role as a **messenger of the gods**, capable of conveying divine information with agility and precision.

Nabu was the **keeper of knowledge**, the one who governed the art of writing, studies, and communication, elements fundamental to the growth and evolution of Chaldean society. His influence extended not only to sacred knowledge, but also to practical areas such as **trade** and diplomacy, areas where quick thinking and clarity of expression were vital to the progress and well-being of the community.

Mercury was thus the celestial symbol of this lively and dynamic energy, capable of **transmitting divine decrees** and fostering the circulation of knowledge. His every appearance and disappearance from the sky was a sign of change and movement: new ideas, new opportunities for exchange and learning, but also a warning of possible quick turns or sudden decisions. **Nabu** and Mercury's influence was crucial to the management of information and intellectual resources, shaping the fate not only of individuals but of society as a whole.

Nergal and Mars

Nergal, the god of war, pestilence and the underworld, was closely related to **Mars**, the red planet that shone in the sky with a fiery, eerie light. **Mars'** sanguine coloring made it the perfect symbol for the destructive and fierce nature of **Nergal**, the bringer of chaos and death. When Mars became visible in the night sky, the Chaldeans saw it as a sign of **impending war**, pestilence, or disaster that would disrupt the world of men.

Nergal was not a god who brought war for the sake of victory, but embodied the necessary destruction, the purifying fire that came upon those who were to be punished or redeemed through suffering. **Mars**, with its fiery light, called to mind bloody battles and the divine fury that was poured out on the battlefield and in the plagues that decimated populations.

When **Mars** ruled the sky, Chaldean priests performed **propitiatory rites**, prayers and sacrifices to try to appease **Nergal**'s wrath. Its omens left no room for benevolent interpretation; it represented conflict, destruction and the need to prepare for dark times. Mars thus became a celestial symbol of warning, a manifestation of the implacable will of Nergal, the lord of death and the underworld, whose wrath could only be tempered with respect and devotion.

Sin and the moon

Sin, the moon god, was a central figure in the Chaldean pantheon and in the daily life of the Mesopotamian people. His reign stretched across the night sky, and his bright lunar face marked the rhythm of life and time. **Lunar phases**, regulated by Sin, controlled the **monthly calendar**, determining auspicious times for sowing, harvesting, and sea-related activities. Each lunar phase had special significance, and its visibility in the sky influenced crucial decisions.

To the Chaldeans, **Sin** was not only the lord of night, but also **the measurer of time**, the one who kept track of the passage of days and months. Its phases guided the planning of **religious festivals**, agricultural rites and sacred ceremonies, linking the earthly world with celestial energies. **The crescent moon** was seen as signaling new beginnings, growth and prosperity, while the **waning moon** suggested times of reflection and closure.

Sin's visibility and phases also influenced important moments in personal life, such as **marriages** and business ventures. Consulting the moon before making decisions was a common practice, as it was believed that Sin could illuminate the right path and protect those who acted in tune with its rhythm. **Sin** represented stability and guidance in the dark, a constant force that accompanied the Chaldeans in navigating life's challenges.

As **the illuminator of the night**, Sin was revered not only as a guardian of the sky, but also as a symbol of wisdom and inner vision, able to reveal hidden secrets during the darkest hours.

Shamash and the sun

Shamash, the sun god, was revered as the **divine judge** and the guarantor of justice among men. His **daily journey across the sky** represented constant vigilance and enlightenment, bringing not only physical light but also moral clarity. Each sunrise marked **Shamash's rebirth**, a symbol of hope and renewal, while each sunset was his temporary death, a moment of reflection heralding his inevitable rebirth. This eternal cycle of death and rebirth represented the immutable truth that, despite the darkness of night, the **sun would rise again**, bringing with it warmth, life and justice.

Shamash's influence went far beyond the natural world. **He was invoked in legal matters**, trials and oaths, to ensure that truth prevailed and justice was done. As an **overseer of justice**, Shamash embodied righteousness and fairness, his revealing light unmasking deception and injustice, illuminating the path of truth. Every oath made under the sun of Shamash was a sacred covenant, a pledge that the god himself would oversee.

Shamash was thus much more than a solar deity: he represented the divine force that ensured balance and justice in the human world, whose course was constantly illuminated and supervised by his watchful heavenly eye.

NUMEROLOGY İS MİNDSET

In previous chapters we have traversed the path of the ancient Chaldeans, exploring the history of numerology as a bridge to understanding **Chaldean Numerology**. This journey was not just an exercise in historical learning. **It was the beginning of a profound transformation**. You began to break through the first veil that covers your awareness, to scratch the barriers that limit your mind. It is like breaking an invisible seal, a **rite of passage** revealing new horizons.The planets and deities we talked about are not mere symbols. **They are powerful mental archetypes**.

Each embodies primordial energies, forces that are deeply rooted in your consciousness. Before you can truly understand the numbers, you must allow these images to penetrate your mind, to resonate within you. **Archetypes don't just live in the sky**. They live inside you, in your unconscious, in your DNA, in the ancestral memories you carry with you.

Each archetype, whether **Marduk, Ishtar or Nergal**, is not just a mythological figure. It is a **key**, a door that opens you to a deeper understanding of cosmic energies. These archetypes vibrate in tune with numbers, connecting the spiritual world with matter. **Your mind must first align with these forces** in order to decode the secrets that the numbers hold.

In this chapter, we will go into the exploration of your **mindset**.

Here we will address those beliefs, those blocks that prevent you from fully understanding numerology. **Mindset is a key**: what you believe and what you think about creates the boundaries of your reality. If your thinking remains limited or closed, the energy of numbers will not be able to flow freely within you.

Break those boundaries and prepare your mind to receive what the numbers, and the archetypes, are ready to show you.

How your mind works

Have you ever wondered why some people seem to effortlessly navigate numbers, while others get lost in numbers and formulas?

The answer is simple: **it depends on the kind of mind we use**.

The reason many teachers fail to teach mathematics is that they try to associate abstract concepts with concrete images. In itself, this is not a bad idea, especially when it comes to **imagination**. When we converse, when we think, our mind uses images. **Both the conscious and subconscious parts** use images to communicate, turning our habits and paradigms into emotional anchors that shape our behavior and guide us to our outcomes.

But although the mind is divided into **two dimensions-one** rational and the other irrational-there are two main modes of thinking: **abstract** and **imaginative**. Only a small part of the population really uses abstract thinking. These are the people often considered outside the box, the ones who challenge the norm. **Dyslexics, schemers, outcasts**. These people, often perceived as different, possess a greater ability to operate in the abstract realm, the place where the most revolutionary ideas are born. It is precisely here that esoteric understanding and, if well aligned, even mathematical skills flourish. But here's the secret: **this mindset can be trained**. It is not a gift reserved for a select few. Through training both the rational and subconscious mind, you can develop the ability to think abstractly. **The first step in any esoteric path** should be training for this mindset. It is like preparing your mind to see beyond the veil of reality, to recognize the invisible threads that connect everything. Imagine being able to understand what others do not see, to connect the numbers to the energy flowing through you, to use this knowledge to **guide your sentimental and spiritual path**.

This is the power that resides in abstract thinking: it allows you to go beyond what is visible, to a deeper level of awareness and understanding.

The imaginative mind

Imagination is the beating heart of your mind. It is that part that everyone, consciously or unconsciously, uses every day. Through images, we think, dream, and understand the world around us. But if you have never really trained this ability, if you have not used it consciously, it becomes impossible to access a deeper level, the realm of abstract thought.

Imagine this: **without clear images in your mind, it becomes impossible to truly understand what you are talking or thinking about**. If I tell you a word-like dog, cat, child-immediately your mind conjures up an image. It is an archetypal image, one that resonates with your experiences, your beliefs, your prejudices. Without that inner visual clarity, thinking becomes fuzzy, elusive.

Therefore, **the first step in training your abstract mindset** is to become aware of how your imagination works, how your mind operates.

Now, **imagine your mind as a person**. Visualize a stick figure whose head is divided into two parts: the upper one represents the rational mind, connected to the senses. This part acts as a filter for any external stimulus, separating what you perceive into fragments that the conscious mind can understand. Below this is your subconscious mind, which acts differently. As if by osmosis, **it absorbs information from the rational mind** and retains it, invisible, but powerful.

The subconscious mind is connected to the body of this imaginary figure. Why? Because it is the information, the programs, the habits that reside in your subconscious mind that move your body, that guide your daily actions without your being fully aware of them. Your habits and paradigms are the autopilot of your life. They determine your results: your weight, your fitness, how much you earn, the people you attract and date.

Being **aware of how your mind works** allows you to look at your life from a new perspective. Suddenly, you can **see clearly** what is not working and understand how to reprogram yourself to improve. **Reprogramming your subconscious** mind is like rewriting your story, aligning your mind and body with what you really want.

Start here: observe your mental images, explore them and find out how they influence your behaviors.

The abstract mind

Abstract thought, unlike the imaginative mind, does not feed on visible images. Rather, it moves through **conceptual** connections, linked to symbols or, more precisely, **archetypes**. These archetypes are the invisible essence of images we know, their energetic and symbolic core, resonating with the depths of the soul.

When you begin to venture into the study of esotericism, you are exploring the **subtle and mysterious link between macrocosm and microcosm**, the connection that exists between the universe and the individual, between the stars in the sky and the depths of your being. **To understand this connection**, your mind needs special training. It is no longer enough to see the world with rational eyes or to follow linear logical thoughts. You must immerse yourself in the world of archetypes, because **archetypes are the keys that open the doors to the abstract**.

That's why, in esotericism, **letters, numbers, planets and deities** are linked to archetypes in the form of symbolic images. These symbols are not just decorations-they are powerful tools that speak directly to your subconscious mind and spirit. **Through the study of archetypes**, you begin to see the hidden connections, the invisible links that exist between you and the universe. This allows you to build a deeper understanding of the world around you and your place in it. Without this process of **studying archetypes**, it would be impossible to develop a mathematical or abstract mindset. It would be like trying to read a map without first knowing the symbols on it. Abstract thinking cannot exist without this foundation. Archetypes are the foundation upon which your understanding of the cosmos and your own soul is built, **enabling you to read numbers, symbols and cosmic forces with a clarity beyond logical thinking**.

Training your mind in this way means **getting in tune with the hidden order of the universe**.

It is not just an intellectual exercise, but a true inner transformation, enabling you to navigate the invisible energies that govern your life.

Negative paradigms affecting your understanding of numbers.

Before we go further on our journey through numerology, we must take an important step, one that many people overlook. **Your mind**, like soil that must be prepared before planting, must be cleared of those **negative biases** that could undermine your understanding of numbers and their vibrations.

Think of this moment as a stage of **initiatory nigredo**, the first step in spiritual alchemy. Here, your **old identity-that** tied to old thought patterns, limiting beliefs and negative paradigms-will be destroyed to make way for a **new version of yourself**, more open, aware and ready to receive the wisdom of numbers.

Negative paradigms are like invisible chains. They block your ability to see numbers for what they really are: powerful symbols that connect the microcosm and the macrocosm. Perhaps you have always thought that numbers are cold, logical, hard to understand, or that math is not your forte. These are just reflections of beliefs that do not really belong to you, but which you have absorbed over time.

To free yourself from these chains, you must immerse yourself in a process of **mental reprogramming**. It is not enough just to read or understand concepts; you must make this new mindset your own, internalize it until it becomes part of you. Repeat each positive paradigm at least **five times a day for a month**. Repetition and immersion are the keys. It is like rewriting the code of a program, line by line, until the old version no longer exists.

In this process, you are not simply changing the way you think. **You are creating a new you**. Every time you repeat these new beliefs, you are chiseling away the remnants of your old identity, the one that doubted its own power, the one that thought numbers were just empty digits.

Numbers are much more than that. They are **energetic keys** that can open doors in your emotional, spiritual and personal life. But to use them, you must first align your mind with their vibrations. **Each negative paradigm you leave behind** brings you closer to a deeper understanding and a new version of yourself, ready to navigate the hidden symbols of the universe.

numerology to win the lottery is foolish.

Many people approach numerology with the idea that they can **win the lottery ticket**, looking for a quick and magical way to change their finances. But if these people truly understood the power and meaning of numbers, they would know that **the mathematical probability** of winning the lottery is almost nonexistent: **1 in a billion**. To keep hoping for this outcome is like chasing a mirage in the desert.

Behind this attitude lies a deeper problem: **a toxic relationship with money**. People who approach numerology with these expectations often **live in scarcity**, convinced that money is something limited that only those who cheat or cheat can obtain. This belief leads them to fall into a cycle of self-sabotage. Even when they manage to get some money, **they immediately squander** it, justifying themselves by saying that they are "reinvesting" it, when in fact they are just trying to win again.

This mentality not only ruins their economic life, but **also undermines their personal and spiritual success**. The toxic relationship with money is reflected in every aspect of their existence, blocking the possibility of growth and driving away prosperity. If you cannot change the way you think about money, **you will never be able to attract it** in a healthy and consistent way.

Money is not a fixed, limited object reserved for the few. It is an energy, an instrument of exchange. Exactly as sugar molecules exchange energy within the body, so money is a means of exchanging value. And do you know what the secret is? Money is **infinite and easily obtained**. Every day more is printed, every day new money-making opportunities emerge. You don't need a title or a windfall to get money. **You only need to produce value.**

And producing value means **helping people improve their lives**, exactly as I am doing with you, explaining these concepts. When you focus on how you can offer value to others, money flows naturally. Write on a piece of paper every day, "**Money is infinite and easily obtained.**" Let this statement seep into your mind, transforming your relationship with the energy of money.

Change your mindset and you will see how the numbers will guide you to a new understanding, where **personal and financial success** is not a matter of luck, but of alignment with cosmic energies.

You are good at math

If you keep telling yourself otherwise, that you are not good at something, that you do not deserve success, you are only **reinforcing an invisible wall** between you and what you desire. Every time you formulate a negative thought, you are unknowingly creating a barrier that keeps you from your potential. But you can choose to change this dynamic.

Instead of saying, "I'm not good at this," ask yourself, **"How can I get better at this?"** This small change in your perspective can open a door toward improvement. **It doesn't stunt your growth**, but pushes you toward self-improvement. Whenever you ask yourself this question, your mind starts looking for solutions instead of locking itself into a downward spiral.

Negative repetition is insidious. Think about this for a moment: the average person is constantly bombarded with depressing messages. A study conducted by Dr. Vitale in the United States revealed that we are exposed to about **700 negative phrases a day**.

We hear them in the family, at work, on TV, on social media. And if you add to this daily bombardment the negative voices from your past, such as those from school, the picture becomes even heavier.

But here comes the crux: **you are not to blame**. You probably had teachers who were unable to teach you math. **They were unable to show you how your mind really works**, and they transferred the burden of their failure onto you. If in a class of 30 children only 2 understand math, the problem is not you. It is the teacher who has failed to adapt, and math itself confirms this for us. **It is not you who is incapable**; you have been conditioned to accept a false reality.

When a teacher tells you that you are not good, this statement becomes ingrained in your subconscious, creating a **limiting paradigm**.

But now that you understand how your mind works, now that you know the power of abstract thinking, **you have all the tools to be good too**. Not just good, but **better** than those who never had access to this knowledge.

Start telling yourself every day, **"I'm good at math."** Change the narrative that has been imposed on you. Your mind is a most powerful tool, capable of adapting and learning, of growing and improving. And now, with the knowledge you have gained, you are ready to rewrite your destiny, step by step.

CHALDEAN NUMBERS

In the previous chapter, we walked together on an intense and necessary path: **the destruction of old paradigms**. This work, challenging as it is, is essential to free your mind from the prejudices that block your deep understanding of numbers. Without this initial purification, it would be impossible for you to access the more advanced levels of numerology, such as symbolic interpretation and, later, the complex calculations that bring this ancient knowledge to life.

For some of my students, despite the simplifications I have introduced in previous texts, the approach to Chaldean numerology proved to be hostile. **Old thought patterns** kept them anchored in a limited vision, unable to grasp the power of numbers and apply them to their own lives. But you bravely faced this process of destruction and rebirth. **We cleansed your mind together**, removing the dirt that years of wrong teachings and external conditioning had deposited in its depths.

Now, thanks to this work, you are ready to build your knowledge on a **solid foundation**, as sturdy as a temple built to last. With the tools you have acquired, you not only understand the meaning of numbers, but you perceive them on a symbolic and archetypal level.

Your subconscious has been reprogrammed to welcome this new knowledge and be guided by numerological wisdom, abandoning past limitations.

This esoteric work, a real **manipulation of the subconscious**, made you able to access the symbolic language of numbers.

Now, through mental imagery and repetition, numbers are no longer empty digits, but **keys** that open invisible doors, connecting you to subtle energies, to deep connections between your being and the world around you.

You are ready to immerse yourself in this universe. From here on, the Chaldean numbers will not just be concepts; they will become **tools of transformation**, mirrors that reflect your path and the energy around you.

Chaldean Number 1: The Influence of the Sun and the Blessing of Shamash

Imagine walking under the midday sun, feeling its pure and unstoppable energy on your skin. This is the power of the **number 1** according to Chaldean tradition, a number that carries with it the essence of the Sun and the divine influence of **Shamash**, the god of justice and truth. In this ancient tradition, the Sun was not only a star in the sky, but a source of spiritual illumination and universal order. The number 1, as a manifestation of this primordial light, is a symbol of **leadership, independence and a burning desire for freedom**.

When the number 1 accompanies you, you are called to embody a force that knows no uncertainty. It is a flame that cannot be extinguished, a light that admits no rival. Your soul recognizes itself as unique, as the starting point. There is nothing casual about your presence, and your every step seems guided by an instinct that always leads you forward, never backward. You are like a ray of light, able to shed clarity where others see only darkness. **Your path is never ordinary, but that of a pioneer, a guide**. And this role is not without challenges: being the first also means facing the deepest shadows alone.

The number 1 stands for creation and beginning. Just like the Sun rising at dawn, bringing the day, you too feel the call to lead the way. This power to begin, to initiate, is a rare quality that does not belong to everyone. It is the power of a soul that knows it can change the course of its life. You are destined to create, to open new paths, to break the chains of the past. This number gives you a **firm, almost unwavering will**: when you decide on something, your determination becomes an armor, protecting you from doubts and insecurities.

The number 1 is also the symbol of absolute independence. Just as the Sun does not need anything to shine, you also do not feel the need to depend on others. Your autonomy is your strength, a quality that few can fully understand. It is a kind of ancestral call, a deep vibration that urges you to walk on your own, to discover the world according to your own vision, not that of others. **This does not mean being alone, but choosing to be the author of your own destiny**.

Shamash, the god who represents this number, is also the lord of justice. In you, this energy translates into a strong sense of fairness, of what is right and wrong. You do not tolerate injustice or impositions. Being under the influence of the Sun and Shamash makes you naturally refractory to any form of submission: you cannot stand for others to decide for you, and you are not afraid to stand up for your beliefs, even if it means being a voice out of the choir. **Your soul, imbued with the light of Shamash, is called to shine with a light that is not only personal, but universal**. Your presence is often a challenge to those who seek to harness you or limit your freedom.

But this independence comes at a price. Your aversion to authority, this desire to be the authority yourself, can bring you up against obstacles that require patience, diplomacy, and sometimes compromise. While your nature drives you to be free and untamed, there are also situations when the world demands your ability to adapt. It is in these moments that No. 1 becomes a master of wisdom, teaching you the virtue of calm. This is the greatest challenge: **finding the right balance between your freedom and the boundaries imposed by reality**. It is not easy for you, but it is the price of a soul that was born to be autonomous.

In love, the number 1 carries with it an aura of magnetism and strength. You are attracted to those who share your desire for freedom, those who respect your individuality without trying to change it. **For you, love is never a cage, but a dance of free souls**. However, this need for independence can also become an obstacle, especially if the other person cannot understand your need for space and autonomy. Love, for you, is like a reflection of the Sun: beautiful, dazzling, but never static. You are attracted to souls who, like you, are not afraid to shine alone, who are not intimidated by your intensity, but find inspiration and strength in it.

Being under the influence of the Sun also means being constantly exposed to its shadow. Shamash, with its unyielding justice, leaves no room for compromise. And so, while shining in your own light, you are also invited to confront the more hidden sides of your personality. The desire for independence can turn into loneliness; inner strength can become rigidity. **This is where your soul must face its dark side**, discover what lies behind the need to always be the first, always the strongest. This number asks you to be honest with yourself, to accept your frailties without fear, to allow your light to touch even your insecurities. Number 1 also invites you to take your power of initiative outward, into the world. It is not enough to shine on your own: you have the task of enlightening others as well, of guiding them on a path of growth. Shamash, the Sun god, shines not only for himself, but for all who seek truth. You, too, like him, are called to be a beacon, to spread your knowledge, your energy. Your natural leadership is not only a gift to you, but a gift to those around you. **You have the ability to inspire, to awaken others**; you can lead them to see their own light, to recognize their own power.

You are destined to become an example of strength and integrity. Yet, you will not always find companions along your path. Many will be intimidated by your intensity; others will try to hold you back, to take you down with them. But you were born to rise again, to overcome any difficulty. Number 1 asks you to have the courage to be different, not to give in to the temptation to fit in. **Being yourself will be your greatest victory**. And whenever you have doubts or fears, remember: the Sun always rises, even after the darkest night.

Ultimately, the number 1 brings you to know the truth of who you are. It is a number that admits no compromise, a symbol of **absolute authenticity**. To be under this influence is to live with purpose, with a clear direction. Your every action is guided by an awareness of who you are and what you can become. The Sun, with all its light, knows no shadows. So too you are called to live without hiding, leaving nothing unsaid. Your soul, illuminated by Shamash, is destined to shine.

Chaldean Number 2: The Influence of the Moon and the Blessing of Sin

Imagine the glow of the full moon on a silent night, when the air seems charged with secrets and everything is pervaded by a muffled, almost dreamlike atmosphere. **This is the essence of Chaldean Number 2**. In this number there is the delicacy of the Moon, its soft, enveloping flow that speaks directly to the heart. In fact, the Moon does not emit its own light, but reflects that of the Sun: and so those influenced by the number 2 have a soul capable of reflecting and amplifying the emotions of others, of feeling every nuance with intensity. It is a magic that not everyone can understand, and it carries with it as much a blessing as a challenge.

Under the influence of the Chaldean lunar god, **Sin**, the number 2 represents the silent force of empathy and inner connection. Sin was the god who observed the cycles of the Moon, the one who guided the stages of growth and decline that affect not only the outer world but also the depths of the soul. The number 2, like the Moon, grows and retracts, ebbs and flows. People who carry this energy embody a sensitivity that makes them deeply perceptive. They can pick up on what is unspoken, understand hidden emotions. **This is their strength, but also their mystery**, because those who are so connected to the Moon may find themselves living between dream and reality, between intuition and material reality.

Your soul, when influenced by this number, is similar to a watercolor painted on a body of water: beautiful in its transparency, capable of reflecting every nuance around it. But this same quality can make you vulnerable, precisely because **your ability to feel is so intense that you often get lost in emotional details**. You can understand others on a level beyond words, as if you can hear their heart through yours. Yet, this empathic ability can make you forget about yourself, what you really want and what makes you happy. Sometimes, you feel the need to hide, to retreat into silence, because the emotions you sense around you become almost unbearable.

The wearer of the number 2 is often a silent spiritual guide, a presence that inspires confidence and can listen without judging. But while you can be the refuge of others, giving comfort and understanding, you may find it difficult to receive the same kind of support. **Your gentleness may be perceived as weakness**, and those who don't know you thoroughly may not understand your true inner strength. This is one of the great dilemmas of Number 2: being seen as fragile, when in fact you possess a resilience of steel, forged in the fire of the soul. Sin, the moon god, gives you a soft light, but this light is sometimes in danger of being obscured by those who are unable to see beyond the surface.

Your creativity, like the energy of the Moon, is deep and introspective. There is something magical and melancholy about what you create, as if your art is a channel for expressing those emotions that you cannot always put into words. The Moon, with its phases, teaches you that beauty can be ephemeral and that there is strength even in vulnerability. **Your art, your creative expression, has the power to touch the souls of others**, to evoke hidden feelings and bring to light what would normally remain in the shadows. This talent is valuable, but not always recognized; it requires the courage to put yourself out there and the patience of someone who knows that his or her worth does not depend on external recognition.

However, the lunar sensitivity that accompanies you can also become a trap. **Your mind is like a canvas on which every emotion is powerfully imprinted,** leaving traces that can become scars. You may find yourself mulling over small details, words said or unsaid, glances and nuances that others don't even notice. This tendency to dwell on details makes you an exceptional person at catching what others miss, but it can also lead you to lose sight of the big picture, to feel lost in a maze of feelings and impressions.

In love, the number 2 envelops you with a deep desire for connection, for genuine intimacy. You are not attracted to superficial relationships; for you, love is a sacred art, a meeting of souls. **You seek a partner who can be a mirror for your soul**, someone who can understand you without the need for words, appreciate your gentleness and reflect your depth. But the risk is that your tendency to give without reservation will leave you feeling empty, especially if the other person is unable to give you the same intensity. At times, you may feel like the Moon shining in solitude, visible yet distant. Your soul longs for fusion, connection, but at the same time fears loss of self.

The influence of the god Sin teaches you to look beyond appearances, to seek the truth hidden in the hearts of others. You are a person who can understand the nuances of life, who sees shadows and light as parts of a single dance. **However, it is essential that you learn to protect your energy**, not to let your sensitivity consume you. This is a precious gift, but one that requires discernment. The Moon can be seductive and hypnotic, but it can also induce you to get lost in the depths of the unconscious, to stray into worlds made of dreams and illusions.

The biggest challenge for you under the influence of the number 2 is learning to maintain a balance between your inner world and outer reality. **Being the Moon number means being able to navigate emotions without being overwhelmed by them**. Your strength lies in your ability to love, to understand, to heal. But it is necessary that you also find your center, that you do not lose sight of who you really are. Like the Moon reflecting the light of the Sun, you too must learn to reflect without absorbing everything. Being empathetic does not mean taking on someone else's pain, but knowing how to understand it without allowing it to affect your essence.

Your soul needs spaces of silence, moments to retreat to regain your energy. You should not be afraid to say no, to close doors when you feel the need to protect yourself. **Learning to set boundaries is an act of love toward yourself**. Those who truly love you will understand and respect this need of yours, and will be able to approach you without violating your sacred space.

The number 2, with all its delicacy, is a powerful number precisely because of its ability to sense what others miss. Sin, the lunar god, guides you with a soft light, a light that is reflection and insight, a light that does not dazzle but reveals hidden truths. Your soul is like a river that flows placidly but has an underground force, an invisible current that never stops. Never forget this force of yours, even when the world seems too harsh, even when you feel you are misunderstood.

Being a person with the number 2 means dancing to the rhythm of the Moon, following its cycles, accepting its variations. Your soul is made of **light and shadow, empathy and introspection**, love and loneliness. Do not try to change this essence of yours, do not fear your sensitivity. You are destined to illuminate the world with a light that does not belong to everyone, a light that belongs to those who can see with their hearts.

Chaldean Number 3: Jupiter's Influence and the Blessing of Marduk

Imagine Jupiter, the giant of the heavens, with its immense aura radiating strength and abundance. At the heart of the number 3 lies the very energy of this mighty planet, a drive toward expansion and personal fulfillment that you can feel within you like a fire that never goes out. Under the guidance of the Chaldean deity **Marduk**, god of justice and prosperity, the number 3 calls for growth that does not stop at mere earthly ambitions. **Marduk was the god who, according to ancient beliefs, gave order to chaos**, and those influenced by the number 3 carry with them this desire to bring light and clarity, to expand into new horizons.

If your number is 3, then a force lives in you that seems impossible to contain. You have an inner energy that pulses, always seeking new goals, new challenges, new lands to explore. Expansion is not just something you desire; it is a necessity, it is the call of Jupiter, that imposing planet that accepts no limits. **You feel within you the urge to grow and explore**, to conquer spaces that others fear to cross. It is a drive that can make you feel like a rushing river, impossible to stop. You have the ambition to make a mark, not to go unnoticed.

Marduk urges you to become a symbol of strength and prosperity, but he also asks you to face your shadows, to bring order where there is chaos, within and without you. This is the gift and burden of the number 3: Expansion, in fact, is an immense power, but it must be guided with wisdom. It is not simply a thirst for success or fame; it is a desire to express your potential, to achieve an inner greatness that resonates in every aspect of your life.

Your mind, under the influence of Jupiter, is like a star map that guides you to see beyond the limits of the present. You are a skilled strategist, a person who can organize and plan, but this has a deeper motive: **you want to leave an imprint**, something that others can follow. Indeed, it is not unusual for those influenced by the number 3 to be natural leaders, someone who attracts others with their charisma and confidence. But this is not imposed leadership. It is a power that comes from your ability to expand your vision, to see possibilities where others see only walls.

In love, this energy leads you to desire a connection that goes beyond the mundane and superficial. You are attracted to those who share your thirst for growth, those who have the strength to accompany you on your spiritual and material journeys. **You are not content with a stagnant relationship**; you need someone who is ready to evolve with you, a partner who can keep up with your ambitious dreams. But this can also lead you to experience an inner dualism: on the one hand you long for stability and on the other a constant need for freedom drives you. This is a challenge Jupiter and Marduk pose to you, asking you to strike a balance between the desire to ground yourself and the desire to explore new avenues.

Jupiter's energy, however, also carries with it a warning: expansion, if unguided, can become excessive. **The risk is to want too much, to try to grab everything without appreciating what you already have**. This spirit of conquest can turn into an urge to fill every space in your life without ever giving yourself a break to breathe and enjoy the present. Marduk, the god of order, reminds you that even expansion must have its boundaries, that harmonious growth requires respect for your limits. In other words, he invites you to find an inner discipline that allows you to achieve balance.

The number 3 also carries with it a strong spiritual charge, a connection with the divine dimension of power and justice. Those influenced by this number possess **great confidence in themselves and their ability to manifest what they desire**. But to keep this power pure, it is necessary that the desire for fulfillment not become selfish. You must be ready to expand not only for yourself, but also to inspire and enrich those you meet along the way. This is Marduk's message: a true leader does not seek only her own success, but works to bring light to those around her, to ensure that her own greatness can enlighten others as well.

In the professional sphere, number 3 pushes you toward positions of authority or roles where you can express your organizational skills and natural charisma. **You have a knack for taking** charge, managing projects or teams with a confidence that inspires trust in others. However, because of this very aptitude for leadership, you may have difficulty accepting the authority of others. You often feel inclined to follow your own path rather than obey someone else's rules. This is a sign of an independent mind, of a soul that desires to be its own ruler, as Marduk is the ruler of his kingdom. But sometimes this inclination can lead you to clash with those who do not understand your need for freedom and control.

With your expansive nature, you may also find yourself wanting to embrace too many projects at once, risking dissipating your energy. **Ambition is a powerful weapon, but it must be used wisely**. Jupiter gives you the ability to think big, to see the whole picture, but to realize your potential it is essential that you learn to focus on what really matters, on what brings value to your life and the lives of others. Expansion does not have to become an endless race; sometimes, the greatest power lies in the ability to choose and let go.

Finally, the number 3, as a symbol of growth and abundance, connects you deeply to the principle of manifestation. With your strategic mind and enterprising spirit, you are able to **attract what you desire** into your life, to materialize your visions through determination and faith in your path. But it is crucial that this ability to attract is used consciously. Expanding without wisdom can lead to scattering, while cultivating your dreams with discernment leads to authentic fulfillment.

Jupiter and Marduk's message to you is clear: **Grow, but remember who you are**. Expand, but never lose your center. Conquer the world, but do it with a pure heart and sincere intentions. Jupiter gives you the strength to reach far, to explore unknown territories and to leave a tangible mark, but Marduk urges you not to forget the value of order and harmony.

The number 3 is thus a path of power and wisdom, of expansion and responsibility. **You are called to grow, to conquer, to enlighten**, but also to find ways to stay true to what really matters. This is the challenge and gift of the number 3: a greatness that knows no limits except those you decide to respect yourself. Under the influence of Jupiter and Marduk, you possess the power to create your own destiny, to shape the world with your vision, and to leave a legacy that speaks of you even when you are no longer here.

Chaldean Number 4: The Influence of Uranus and the Blessing of Anu

The number 4 in Chaldean numerology is deeply related to the rebellious and visionary force of Uranus, the planet of the unexpected and progress, which carries with it the disruptive fire of change and innovation. **Uranus is the lord of free spirits**, an energy that never lets itself be bridled by fixed patterns or imposed rules. Bound to him is the Chaldean deity **Anu**, the god of the sky, whose infinite realm holds unexplored mysteries and possibilities that no mortal dares to fully contemplate.

Those influenced by the number 4 embody Anu's vision and challenge. You have an inherent nature that pushes you to look beyond the obvious, to push into territories that others avoid or do not see. You are a free and innovative mind, the bearer of ideas that seem to come out of nowhere, almost as if you are receiving messages from an unseen realm. In every area of your life, Uranus guides you like a rushing wind, fueling in you a deep desire for truth and originality. Yet, this innovative vision can also separate you from others. Individuals with the number 4 are often **misunderstood, perceived as different or even strange** because of their tendency to defy convention. Your uniqueness does not always find appreciation, but it is what makes you essential, a beacon for those ready to embrace new perspectives.

Your connection with Anu, the god of heaven and limitless expansion, makes you a soul who is not afraid to push the boundaries of the known. **Your rebellious spirit makes you uncomfortable for those seeking security and stability**, but it is also what gives you that mysterious and irresistible charm. In love and relationships, you tend to attract those who are fascinated by your depth and uniqueness. **You are not made for**

superficial or conventional loves; you seek a connection that challenges, enriches and expands your own worldview. However, your way of loving may frighten those accustomed to more common forms of affection. Number 4 requires a love that is able to embrace chaos and the unexpected, a partner who understands the beauty of what is different and can walk alongside you without trying to change your essence.

The energy of Uranus, to which you are so deeply connected, drives you to **seek truth, always and everywhere**. You are not satisfied with simple, trite answers; you are willing to dig, to question, to dismantle old beliefs to get at what is authentic. This tendency can lead you into conflict with those around you, especially those who try to impose a rigid and limiting order. You were born to shake the foundations of what is static, and this makes you a transformative force. It is not uncommon for you to feel alone in this battle, but this is precisely where Anu supports you: your solitude is a sacred flame, a call to the open sky, to what is bigger, freer.

In the professional sphere, your ability to think outside the box is an invaluable gift. **You have a vision that few can fully comprehend**, and your mind is like an alchemical laboratory in which new ideas, solutions, and inventions are born. However, the path of those ruled by Uranus is never easy: your ideas often disturb those who are attached to rigid patterns or those who are not ready for radical change.

 You are the kind of person who loves to dismantle traditional systems in order to build new, more just and authentic ones, but this can lead you to clash with those in power who prefer stability to change. This path, which may seem lonely and hostile at times, is actually your calling, your destiny.

Uranus' influence makes you a breakthrough figure, a pioneer. Yet there is a fragility in this struggle of yours for authenticity:

the world is not always ready to embrace what it does not understand. Number 4 carries with it the weight of one who can see beyond, who glimpses possibilities where others see only boundaries.

This gives you an aura of mystery and can lead you to feel misunderstood, even rejected by those who do not accept your way of thinking and being. Yet in spite of everything, you feel inside that your task is precisely to be different, to be the spark that ignites new visions.

In the area of spiritual growth, number 4 offers you **the ability to perceive what is hidden, to explore dimensions that others avoid**. Uranus is the planet of hidden truths, of sudden revelations, and this makes you especially sensitive to messages coming from deep within your soul and from the universe itself. Under the guidance of Anu, the sky god, you feel called to explore unknown worlds, to seek answers where few have the courage to go. Your spirituality is unconventional, it does not follow set paths; it is a personal, solitary journey that leads you toward the awakening of your soul.

In love, as in life, you tend to desire a connection that understands you without forcing you, that leaves you free to explore and grow. Number 4 is attracted to people who have similar depth, to those who are able to accept your independence without suffocating you. However, your path in love is not an easy one: you are attracted to people who respect your uniqueness, but finding a balance between the need for freedom and the desire to share can be a challenge. You may often wonder if there really is someone who can love you without wanting to change who you are.

The potential of #4 is manifested when you fully accept your uniqueness and make peace with your nonconformist nature.

You were not born to follow the crowd, and therein lies your true power.

Anu guides you toward a realization that goes beyond the boundaries of society, an understanding of yourself that allows you to act with courage and determination, even if it means being misunderstood. You are a rebel of the soul, and your strength lies precisely in your ability to follow your heart, even when it leads you away from the common paths.

Finally, Uranus and Anu's message to you is this: **embrace your destiny as an innovator, a free spirit, a bringer of new truths**. Number 4 gives you the ability to change the world, but to do so you will have to accept your solitary nature, the incessant call to the unknown.

Your path is not easy, but it is full of discoveries, visions, and deep connections to the whole. Uranus teaches you not to be afraid to break with the past, to look beyond appearances, to find the hidden truth in every situation.

Anu, the god of the infinite sky, accompanies you on this journey, inspiring **you to become a beacon for those who are ready to see the light**. You are destined to leave an imprint, to bring change, to elevate your soul to the stars. The number 4 is your seal and your guide, an invitation to discover that the roads less traveled are the ones that lead to the most incredible discoveries.

Chaldean Number 5: Mercury's Influence and the Blessing of Nabu

The number 5, according to Chaldean numerology, is under the fluid and iridescent guidance of Mercury, the planet of adaptability, movement and communication. But not only that. Mercury is the conduit between the world of humans and the world of the gods, and he carries with him the vibrant energy of the Chaldean deity **Nabu**, the god of wisdom and the exchange of ideas. Nabu is the one who can dance between the realms of the visible and the invisible, and **you, bound to the number 5, are his reflection** on this Earth. Like him, you are a messenger, a weaver of connections who flows between people and situations with agility.

Your essence is dynamic, elusive, just like the wind that changes direction without warning. You are a creature in constant motion, a social butterfly dancing from flower to flower, gathering experiences, feelings, stories. There is no place where you cannot feel comfortable-you have the gift of adapting and transforming yourself according to your environment. And if someone tries to hold you back or imprison your free spirit, they soon find that it is impossible. **Number 5 is absolute freedom**, and no chains can stop your desire to explore.

Nabu, god of wisdom and writing, inspires you to use speech as a tool for connection and discovery. **You are a born communicator**. Your words know how to reach people's hearts, creating bridges between different worlds and visions. In love, as in life, this ability of yours makes you irresistible in the eyes of those around you. You are that person who knows what to say and how to say it, able to adapt the tone, the pace, and even the essence of the conversation to tune in to those in front of you. **With the number 5 by your side, you possess the gift of**

communicative empathy, a rare talent that allows you to tune into the emotional world of others.

Yet, there is a deeper side to you, a side that perhaps only you know. Behind your light-hearted appearance and your incessant urge to move, **lies a need for stability and security** that sometimes surprises you. Mercury, as a planet, cannot sit still for long; it needs to run, to explore, to launch into new adventures. But this constant search for new things can make you feel restless, and you may find yourself longing for a refuge, a place to rest and find peace. Perhaps this is why, while longing for independence, you also feel the need for a love that can welcome you and give you stability without imprisoning you.

In love, you are attracted to those who can accept your free and independent side. Those who love No. 5 know that they must be ready to run alongside you, to not hold you back, to make room for you to be who you are. Relationships for you must be a light dance, a continuous exchange, without rigidity or limits. You need someone who understands that your heart is like a sky that changes color every hour of the day. Stability, for you, is not a cage, but rather a safe space to which you can return when you are ready to stop.

The number 5 carries with it the energy of change and transformation. Like Nabu, you move between different realities, shifting from one experience to another without fear. This makes you an extremely versatile person: you can make the best of any situation, seeing possibilities where others see boundaries. **You are a visionary in constant flux**, always ready to embrace the new, to learn something different, to experiment. Nothing stops you, because you know that every experience, positive or negative, enriches you and brings you closer to a greater truth.

In the professional sphere, this ability of yours to adapt is a precious gift. **You never limit yourself to a single perspective**.

While others follow a path already laid out, you create your own path, exploring paths no one had noticed. Your mind is an expanding universe, always looking for new stimuli, new ideas, new horizons. And this makes you a special person, capable of bringing innovation and freshness to any field. You have a natural aptitude for jobs that require creativity and flexibility, such as art, communications, marketing, or any other activity in which you can express your lively spirit and brilliant mind.

Yet, just like Mercury, you need to be careful not to dissipate your energy. **Your thirst for novelty, for discovery, for freedom can sometimes lead you to lose focus**. You may find yourself jumping from one project to another, from one idea to another, without being able to complete what you had started. This is one of the challenges of #5: learning to find balance between the desire to explore and the need to stop, to ground yourself. Nabu teaches you that true power lies not only in moving nonstop, but also in being able to listen to the silence, to savor the moments of pause.

On a spiritual level, the number 5 invites you to explore dimensions beyond the surface. **Your soul is curious, always searching for answers, for hidden truths**. You are never satisfied with conventional explanations: you feel there is always something more, a mystery to be unraveled, a message waiting to be deciphered. Mercury, like Nabu, is the god of messages, the conduit between the visible and the invisible, and this quality of his is reflected in your nature. You are inclined to explore the world of intuition, spirituality, and subtle dimensions. The number 5 urges you to seek the truth in everything, to never stop at first impressions.

In love, as in life, you seek a deep but free connection. Your ideal partner is someone who understands you and can dance with you, without trying to hold you back or limit your spirit. You long for a relationship that is like an endless dialogue, a continuous discovery. Your soul is always on a journey, and you need someone who can appreciate this side of you, without fear of losing you. **Whoever loves number 5 must be ready to share your adventure**, to welcome your changes, to respect your need for freedom.

Mercury and Nabu's message to you is clear: **follow your curiosity, heed the call of change, but don't forget to find a point of balance**. The number 5 is a number of transformation, of movement, of exploration, but also of wisdom. Your challenge is to learn how to combine your ever-evolving nature with a stable base, a firm point to return to when you feel the need to find yourself.

Ultimately, the number 5 is the number of souls on a journey, of those who are not afraid to explore, of those who are always seeking new adventures. Mercury guides you with its lively, intelligent energy, and Nabu inspires you to seek wisdom in every experience, to turn every encounter into a lesson. Your path is unique, different, full of discoveries. Your path will never be boring, and even if you find yourself changing direction often, you will always know how to find yourself again.

Embrace your essence, embrace your desire for freedom, and continue to explore the world with the curiosity of one who knows that every experience carries with it a truth. The number 5 is your seal, your invitation to discover the world with new eyes, to dance among possibilities, to let every encounter, every place, every moment become part of your journey.

Chaldean Number 6: The Influence of Venus and the Blessing of Ishtar

The number 6 in Chaldean numerology vibrates under the charm and influence of Venus, the star of beauty and sensuality, the planet whose radiance seems to whisper promises of harmony, pleasure and attraction in your ear. This venereal energy is not accidental; it encapsulates the link with the Chaldean deity **Ishtar**, goddess of love and war, desire and fertility, a force that can make the number 6 irresistible. Ishtar was known for her ability to bewitch and conquer anyone she met, and those connected with this number often carry within themselves this **magnetic charm** that seems to emanate naturally.

If your number is 6, then you know what it is like to walk into a room and capture attention without even uttering a word. You have a presence that hardly goes unnoticed: others seem drawn to your aura as if by a secret music, something that touches the soul and vibrates the subtlest chords. It is your gift, the power to captivate, to bring balance and beauty, to soften and harmonize. It is not a mere whim of the stars, but an ancient energy that makes you adept at making connections **that touch the heart** and bonds that transcend mere surface appearance.

Being a number 6 also means possessing an innate sense of beauty and grace. This sensibility manifests itself in many forms: from a love of the arts to an ability to appreciate aesthetic details to a natural inclination to surround yourself with objects that make you feel safe and at peace. Venus, in you, is a **desire for serenity and refuge**, but also for passion and conquest. On a romantic level, you have an incredible ability to give yourself to another with dedication and care, but at the same time you manage to make yourself desired, remaining somewhat mysterious, shrouded in a charm that you do not fully grasp. You love, but your love must respect your need for beauty and harmony.

Ishtar is not only the goddess of love, but also of war. This duality flows through you: you can be gentle, loving, a safe haven for those you love, but at the same time you can be determined and, if need be, even relentless. When someone tries to disturb your serenity or threatens what is dear to your heart, you can show surprising strength, a strength that recalls Ishtar's warrior nature.

This dark, powerful and protective side is the secret that makes you fascinating, because few suspect that behind your gentleness lies such a decisive strength.

In the social world, your natural magnetism makes you charismatic. People are attracted to your way of being, your ability to balance between passion and gentleness, between charm and stability.

You know how to use words like delicate arrows to influence others without ever coming across as aggressive. You have a unique ability to make those around you feel at ease, to bring out the best in others simply by your presence. But you also know, and this is the most intriguing side, how to **direct your charm toward your goals**, as if you had an inner compass to guide you, a desire to achieve what you set out to do gracefully, without ever losing control.

This is where the most challenging aspect of the number 6 comes in. **This same capacity for attraction can turn into manipulation**. You are adept at making others see what you want them to see, at guiding their emotions and reactions to achieve your ends. Deep intuition lives in you, a subtle understanding of emotional and psychological dynamics, a gift that, if not used with balance, can drive you to use your power selfishly. This side of #6 warns you against the temptation to get what you want by exploiting the weaknesses of others. Ishtar, after all, is also the goddess of raging passion, and the line between the desire for harmony and manipulation can be thin.

To love a number 6 is to enter a world of contrasts: passion and calm, sweetness and strength. Those who fall in love with you cannot help but feel enchanted, but at the same time they must accept the challenge of winning your heart day after day. You do not settle for superficiality, and lukewarm love is not what you seek. Those who wish to be near you must prove to you that they deserve your affection, that they understand your essence. Yet you, too, sometimes feel the need for someone who can penetrate you deeply, someone who can see beyond the apparent charm and embrace every side of you, even those you yourself struggle to understand.

The number 6 makes you **a companion, a confidante, but also a guide** for those who seek beauty in life. You have the gift of transforming environments, of instilling harmony wherever you go. You are often the person others turn to in times of trouble, for you exude a tranquility that has the power to reassure, to make those around you feel as if they are protected.

And you, after all, love to be this reference figure, this **loving and reassuring center of gravity** for those you hold dear.

However, you must be careful not to sacrifice too much of yourself for the well-being of others. The number 6, with its call to beauty and serenity, may push you to put the needs of others ahead of your own, to sacrifice your own balance to protect those you love. But Venus teaches you that the most authentic love comes not from renunciation, but from balance.

You must learn to say no when you feel someone might take advantage of your goodness, and to remember that your heart also deserves attention, care and respect.

Professionally, number 6 makes you an exceptionally **creative and diplomatic** person.

You are attracted to professions that allow you to express your aesthetic sense, such as design, art, fashion, or interior design. Yet even in business or more traditional professions, you know how to use your charm to create synergy, to make work a more pleasant and harmonious environment. Your influence makes itself felt even without fanfare, bringing positive change and a sense of beauty to situations that seemed dry.

In summary, the number 6 is a hymn to beauty, love and protection. It teaches you that life can be a space of sweetness, serenity and balance, but it also warns you not to forget your inner strength. Ishtar, with her dual nature, reminds you that the power of love is real only when it is accompanied by an awareness of your boundaries, integrity, and worth. **Embrace your venereal nature, let your charm and sweetness touch others, but never sacrifice your essence.**

Ultimately, your journey is a journey to discover true love: that which is born not of dependence or fear, but of strength and freedom.

Chaldean Number 7: The Influence of Neptune and the Blessing of Ea

The Chaldean number 7 is shrouded in the allure of Neptune, the planet of unseen depths and hidden wisdom, an influence that makes this number especially mysterious. **If you feel the call of 7, then you are attuned to the energy of the eternal waters**, which flow silently, unseen, but never inert. Ruled by the deity Ea, the Babylonian god of waters and occult wisdom, the number 7 carries within it the curiosity of the mystic, the thirst for answers that no one else dares to seek, and the subtle perception of what lies hidden between the folds of reality.

To be a number 7 is to perceive the world through a special filter-a veil that lets the visible shine through but cannot conceal the unseen. You are the kind of person who is never satisfied with simple answers, because you sense that there is always something more. A mystery hidden in the words of others, a secret waiting to be revealed in gestures, a message in the shadows of unspoken things. Like Neptune and like Ea, you move gracefully through the world of archetypes, emotions and symbols, and you do so with a naturalness that to others may seem incomprehensible.

7 is the number of introspection, retreat and sacred solitude. **You don't fear solitude; on the contrary, you make it your sanctuary, the place where you can unravel the mysteries of your inner world**. If you are a number 7, you probably often find yourself reflecting at length on what you see and hear, digging beneath the surface of events and words. This depth sometimes makes you an enigmatic figure in the eyes of others, a person who may seem difficult to understand but who, in fact, possesses an uncommon sensitivity.

Intuition is your secret gift, the compass that guides you through the invisible currents of life. You can sense the emotions of others, even when they try to mask them. You can sense hidden intentions and, often, feel a truth emerging long before it manifests itself in the material world. Neptune has given you the ability to see beyond appearances, and your heart and mind can grasp the finer details. This insight is not just a mere feeling, but a true vision, like a flash that reveals to you what lies behind the masks of reality.

But this sensitivity comes at a price. **Your path is often marked by the challenge of understanding what is real and what is illusory**. Neptune, planet of dreams and visions, invites you to explore the boundaries between the real and the false, the tangible and the ethereal. This means you may find yourself wavering, doubting what you perceive, wondering if your intuitions are true or the result of an overactive imagination. The 7th confronts you with this test, prompting you to develop a solid wisdom, a self-confidence that only time and experience can bring. Being a number 7 also means feeling a strong pull toward all that is mysterious and occult. You are attracted to what others avoid or consider forbidden: **esoteric practices, spiritual disciplines, the world of the unconscious and dreams**. Neptune, with its magnetic force, guides you to explore your psyche, decipher the messages of the unconscious, and penetrate the realms of deepest spirituality. You are not a person who stops at the surface of things: you want to know the roots, you want to get to the heart of the mystery, whatever it is. Ea, the god of the deep sea, awakens in you a hunger for sacred knowledge, for forgotten wisdom.

Your connection to spirituality is unique, deep, and often lonely. If you are a number 7, you probably feel that your life path is not entirely conventional. Perhaps you have always felt a slight distance between you and others, as if you perceive life on a different frequency. This detachment is not a lack of love or empathy, but a form of protection, a way of guarding your inner world that is so precious and delicate. The 7 asks you to respect this uniqueness of yours, to accept that your spiritual path may be different from that of others, and that your task is to seek and preserve the truth you have discovered within yourself.

However, **this search for truth and depth can also lead you to a form of isolation**. Your more sensitive and caring view of life than the ordinary one leads you to feel intense emotions, which can make it difficult to share your world with those who cannot fully understand you. Sometimes you will feel lonely, misunderstood, almost as if you are suspended between two worlds: the visible and the invisible. This loneliness, however, is not without meaning. It is the fertile soil in which the 7 plants the seeds of your inner wisdom, of your ability to understand yourself and others with a depth that only a few can reach.

On a practical level, the number 7 makes you a person who seeks knowledge in all its forms. You are drawn to studies, art, philosophy, science and spirituality. You love to observe, listen and gather information, and your approach to life is similar to that of an explorer: you immerse yourself in anything that can offer an answer or a new perspective. **You are interested in anything that can nourish your soul, anything that has deeper meaning**. Although your nature pushes you toward isolation, it is precisely in this retreat that you find your spiritual nourishment.

On a sentimental level, however, the life of a number 7 can be complex. **Your heart is deep, mysterious, and longs for a love that is equally authentic and intense**. You are not interested in superficial relationships; you prefer the truth, even if it hurts, rather than the bittersweet illusion of a love without substance. However, you often meet people who are not ready to descend into the same emotional depth that is natural for you, and this can leave you with a sense of emptiness, of disappointment. You are looking for a kindred soul, someone who can look into your eyes and see beyond, someone who can appreciate your complex nature without trying to change or limit it.

In a relationship, your need for introspection may be seen as distance, but those who truly love you will understand that this is your way of finding yourself. **You do not ask those who love you to fill your gaps, because you know that only you can do that**. But you ask for understanding, you ask for patience and, above all, you ask for respect for your need for silence and personal space. If you find someone who respects this need of yours, you will be able to give a love that goes beyond words, a love that digs deep and transforms.

Finally, number 7 teaches you the value of authenticity and inner consistency. **You are not interested in conforming to others or following a path you do not feel is your own.**

You are here to seek your truth, to build your worldview, and to honor your soul in all its complexity. Neptune guides you, and with him also Ea, the god of the deep waters, invites you not to be afraid to dive into your emotions, your dreams and your intuition. He invites you to explore every aspect of your existence, without fear of losing touch with reality, for only then can you find your true essence. Number 7, then, is an invitation to **follow your heart, to fearlessly explore the mystery of the soul**. It is a promise that even if your path is lonely, it is rich in meaning and valuable revelations.

Your journey is that of an explorer of the spirit, a seeker who never stops, because she knows that the real treasure is hidden deep within, and that its light is destined to shine, even if only for a chosen few.

Chaldean Number 8: Saturn's Influence and Ninurta's Blessing

The Chaldean number 8 is enveloped in the austere and powerful charm of Saturn, the lord of structure, discipline, and wisdom gained through experience. Ruled by the Chaldean deity Ninurta, the god of justice and daring deeds, 8 embodies the essence of determination, perseverance and authority. Those marked by this number do not walk on easy paths, but feel the call of onerous tasks and great responsibility. **To be an 8 is to accept a destiny of trials**, of challenges that forge character, and of goals that, if achieved, can leave an indelible mark on the world.

Saturn's influence transforms the 8 into a builder, an architect of the solid foundation, who knows that to raise something lasting he must start from the roots. People connected to this number are often the ones who take on the responsibilities that others run away from. They know what it means to sacrifice for a cause, for a project, for a goal, and they devote themselves to it with unwavering determination. It is not just ambition, but a deep sense of **duty to oneself and one's path**. To be an 8 is to understand that true strength comes from overcoming one's limitations, going beyond one's fears and building something tangible, something real.

The 8 carries with it a magnetic appeal, **a strength that does not need to be flaunted, because it is rooted in a deep sense of integrity**. People marked by this number do not seek approval or applause, because their satisfaction lies in the completion of their task, not in accolades. Saturn teaches them that true power is not loud, but quiet and persistent, a fire that burns slowly but never dies out. This perseverance is what makes the number 8 a natural leader, someone whom others look up to with admiration and respect, though often at a distance, intimidated by the intensity of his aura.

Those who resonate with the energy of 8 know that **every step forward is hard-earned**, that nothing in life is given for free, and that true successes require sacrifice. Often, these people face challenges that seem unfair or disproportionate, almost as if fate itself is testing them. But this is precisely Saturn's secret gift: trials are not meant to discourage, but to fortify, to forge a soul capable of endurance and triumph. **Ninurta**, Saturn's Chaldean deity, symbolizes this energy of struggle and resilience: he is the god who goes down to the battlefields and returns victorious, an example of tenacity for anyone who feels drawn to the number 8.

Thus, the number 8 represents a balance between authority and responsibility. **To be an 8 means to embody the principle of authority not to dominate but to lead, not to control but to build**. Those who belong to this energy understand that the true leader is the one who takes on the burden of decisions, who is ready to step up when others hesitate, and who knows how to keep calm in the most turbulent storms. People influenced by the 8 are like rocks: stable, unchanging, able to withstand the winds and storms without wavering.

In love, the path of those marked by the number 8 is not easy. **Their heart is as disciplined as their mind**, and they do not open easily to emotion. They are cautious, reserved, and often find themselves caught between the desire for connection and the fear of losing control. Those who love an 8 must be patient, respect their time, and understand that every opening is an act of earned trust, a gift that requires reciprocity and loyalty. 8s do not like superficial relationships; they prefer stability, commitment, and are looking for someone with whom they can build a solid, deep connection.

But **Saturn always requires a** price, and its price is patience, tolerance, and the ability to endure moments of isolation and introspection. The 8 is not immune to solitude; indeed, solitude is often their sanctuary, the place where they recharge, where they reflect on their actions and reconnect with their purpose. Those with 8 as their guiding number feel driven to improve, to reach their highest version, and they know that to do so they must confront themselves, face their shadows and accept their frailties.

The number 8 is also a symbol of **material stability and abundance**. These people are often attracted to professional and financial success, not out of mere ambition, but because they see prosperity as a form of security and freedom. Saturn's discipline guides them in this direction, teaching them that every accumulated resource must be used wisely, that every gain is the fruit of diligent and careful work. However, this desire for stability can also turn into a trap, as the fear of losing what has been built can generate anxiety and fear of change.

Finally, being an 8 means accepting that one's life will be a **journey of continuous transformation**, in which every obstacle is an opportunity to grow and strengthen oneself. The authority of the 8 is never taken for granted; it is earned day by day, through thoughtful choices and consistent actions. The success of an 8 is not a fortuitous event, but the result of unrelenting perseverance, an ability to endure even when everything seems to be going against you.

Saturn, with its stern and unyielding energy, teaches the number 8 that **true power lies in resilience**. The 8 learns to master themselves, to rule their emotions and discipline their minds, not out of selfishness, but out of a desire to be a stable and reliable force for those they love. Ninurta inspires them to become warriors of their own lives, to fight their own inner battles and to never give up on their own path, no matter how difficult or uncertain it may be.

For those who resonate with the 8, the key to their destiny is to understand that every challenge is a test, every defeat a lesson, and every victory a step toward greater fulfillment. Their mission is to learn to trust themselves, to build relentlessly, and to use their power with wisdom and compassion. **Being an 8 means finding a balance between ambition and humility**, between strength and vulnerability, between external authority and inner peace.

In the end, the number 8 represents a journey that leads to self-knowledge, a journey in which true wealth is within and in which true victory is the ability to remain true to who one is, without compromise. And so, under the guidance of Saturn and Ninurta, the 8 moves forward, knowing that every obstacle makes them stronger, every mistake wiser, and every step, however difficult, brings them closer and closer to their authentic essence.

Chaldean Number 9: The Influence of Mars and the Blessing of Nergal

The Chaldean number 9, illuminated by the impetuous force of Mars, is the vibration of warriors and souls fighting for justice. This number resonates with courage, integrity and a tireless energy that drives those touched by it to look at life as a challenge to be faced, a mission to be accomplished. **To be a 9 is to embody the courage of those who are not afraid of confrontation**, those who do not back down when it is time to speak the truth or take a stand to defend what is right. Those who have 9 as their guiding number move between passion and will, between the impulse to act and the desire to protect.

Mars, planet of fire and war, profoundly influences this issue. And with Mars there is also **Nergal**, the Chaldean god of destruction and rebirth, the deity who guides warriors on the path of life and in their struggles against their own shadows. This juxtaposition makes the number 9 an extraordinary force, capable of transforming reality with its own hands. There is no room for mediocrity: the 9 lives intensely, driven by an inner flame that burns indomitably.

The energy of the number 9 is bold, always ready to push the limits, to probe the boundaries of what is possible. **The life of a 9 is a continual test of character**: he is called to walk difficult paths, to fight for his ideals, and to remain true to what he feels is true and right. Those born under this vibration possess a will of steel and a determination that makes them capable of overcoming even the toughest challenges. They are not content with passive roles, but always seek to be protagonists, to make their mark.

For those who feel the influence of the 9th, **justice is not just an abstract ideal, but a personal mission**. These are people who love just battles, who are not afraid to raise their voices against injustice. Indeed, they draw energy from the struggle itself, as if every obstacle is a push toward their own evolution. Nergal, the deity associated with Mars, represents the will to transform and overcome oneself: he is the god who destroys in order to regenerate, who digs deep to bring truth to light.

The presence of the 9 in one's life involves a journey of challenges and rebirth. **These individuals are not afraid to break with the past**, to destroy what no longer resonates with their essence, and to rebuild on a more authentic basis. They are ready to burn bridges with the past in order to move forward, driven by a thirst for truth and authenticity that cannot be ignored. This call for continuous transformation is one of the most powerful characteristics of the number 9: those who carry it know that nothing is permanent, that life is an unceasing stream of change.

In love, the number 9 can be an overwhelming force. Those who resonate with this energy love intensely, without reservation, and often give themselves completely to their partner. However, their impulsive and passionate nature can make them difficult to understand and manage. They cannot stand half-measures, either in love or in friendship. If they love, they do so with their whole heart; if they turn away, it is because they perceived a lack of sincerity or respect. A 9 needs a partner who can embrace their intense and passionate nature, who is willing to stand by them in the challenges of life.

The lesson of #9 is, in fact, **learning to balance strength and compassion**. Mars teaches to fight, to never give up, but at the same time requires the warrior to also develop a deep sensitivity to humanity. The true 9 is not just a fighter, but a defender of truth, a paladin who knows how much the power of justice can change lives, bringing light where before there was only darkness. This compassionate aspect is a precious gift for those who carry the energy of the number 9, because it allows them to balance their determination with a deep empathy for others.

Nergal, like Mars, embodies the dark and light side of the number 9. **He is not only the god of war, but also of healing through destruction**. For the 9, this duality is crucial: learning to use one's strength not only for oneself, but to create a positive impact in the world. Those living under the influence of this number can often find themselves in roles that require a great sense of responsibility and integrity: leaders, lawyers, activists, teachers. Any field that allows them to put their energy into the service of others is a natural space in which they flourish.

The number 9 is also a symbol of karma, a reminder to follow one's path without fear of consequences, knowing that every action leaves an imprint. For those marked by this vibration, the concept of karma is not just a cosmic law, but a moral guide that spurs them to live authentically, to be true to their word and to stand firm in their values. The 9 knows that what one gives to the world will come back, which is why he always tries to act righteously, even when circumstances seem to play against him.

The essence of the 9 is a flame that burns and transforms. **It is the strength of the spiritual warrior**, who fights not for himself but for a greater cause, one that goes beyond ego and beyond the need for recognition. Those who embody the number 9 feel the call to act for the collective good, to defend the weakest, to fight for those who cannot defend themselves. And in this to find one's purpose, one's truth.Finally, the energy of the number 9 is a journey of inner discovery, an ongoing challenge that leads those touched by it to discover their own depths and confront their own shadows. The number 9 teaches that **true strength is**

not only physical, but above all spiritual. The warrior of 9 is one who knows that courage is not the absence of fear, but the ability to move forward despite fear. It is an energy that asks to let go, to sacrifice the ego for a higher purpose, and to be ready to be reborn whenever life calls for it.

Under the influence of Mars and Nergal, Number 9 becomes a driving force that defies limits, pushing into the unknown with a steadfast heart and a clear mind. Its path is made up of challenges, confrontations and victories, but also moments of introspection and newfound peace. Being a 9 means living intensely, it means looking at life with bold eyes, never bowing down, but always ready to get back up. Their destiny is that of warriors, truth-seekers, free spirits who find, in the balance between strength and compassion, their true greatness.

NUMEROLOGİCAL CALCULATİONS USİNG THE CHALDEAN SYSTEM

One of the greatest challenges when embarking on the journey into Chaldean numerology is **understanding the secret language of numbers**. Perhaps you have already begun to explore this fascinating world, but have felt confused, lost in calculations and formulas, failing to grasp the true power that numbers can have on your life. Many novice students find themselves at this very point. Chaldean numerology is not just a system of counting; it is an astral language, a code that connects numbers to cosmic energies, to unseen worlds, to your very essence. But how to interpret such a complex system? **How to make sense of the numbers** if you do not know their deep spirit, their astral meaning? And how could they guide you if you do not yet know what you are really looking for?

It is easy to fall into the mistake of focusing only on calculations, sums, and techniques that allow you to apply the numerological system, forgetting that every number carries within it a vibration that must be felt and understood before it is measured. Many of the "fuffa gurus" who flock to this field stop at numbers as if they were only computational tools, ignoring the spiritual dimension. But what can a number offer you if you do not know its deeper meaning? **How can you decipher your destiny or find answers in esotericism** if you don't know how to make numbers resonate in your soul?

That is why I have chosen to take you by the hand, slowly, into the heart of Chaldean numerology. Before we get into the calculations, we will explore together the soul of each number. Each number has its own energy, connected to a planet, to an ancient deity, to a specific vibration. It is only by understanding the breath of the numbers that you can truly apply Chaldean numerology to your life. **The numbers speak, but only if you are ready to listen to them**. Throughout this journey, you will not just find formulas or calculation methods. You will find guidance that reveals, step by step, **how to interpret the esoteric implications of each number**. You will discover that numbers, in fact, are like portals that can open your consciousness to greater truths. You will learn to feel each number as a presence, a symbol that vibrates in you and resonates with your experience. It is as if each number can tell you a piece of yourself, illuminate your paths and whisper where to go. This is not the numerology you find in conventional manuals. **Here, the numbers become companions on your journey**. Imagine each number as a star in your inner sky, illuminating the paths of your soul. Before measuring, you must feel. Before you add, you must listen. Each number represents a cosmic energy, and understanding it will help you bring light into the shadows of your life. The Chaldean system is older than you can imagine. It carries with it the knowledge of the priests and astrologers, of those who lived in communion with the stars and planets. **Numbers, according to the Chaldeans, are messengers**. Each number contains a specific message, a hidden truth. When you begin to see numbers in this way, you realize that they are not just tools for making predictions or trying to understand the future. Numbers become keys, opening inner doors, revealing secrets that you yourself may have been unaware you were guarding.

ibration and esotericism of numbers

Have you ever sensed the hidden vibration you give off just by saying your name? Every time you do, you activate a melody of esoteric energies, a set of vibrations that bind to you like an invisible signature. **In Chaldean numerology, each name has a unique frequency**, a resonance that tells who you are and what you bring with you into the world.

This ancient numerology is not limited to numbers and calculations; it goes much further, exploring the link between the microcosm-your inner being-and the macrocosm-the universe and its laws. **Numbers are not just mathematical symbols: they are fragments of stars and planets**; they carry astrological virtues that are imprinted in names and letters. This makes your name not just a set of letters, but a kind of magical talisman that constantly vibrates, infusing you with its virtues and powers.

Esotericism has always studied this connection between the big and the small, between the vast universe and the intimate world of each of us. **Each number represents a celestial force** that influences not only your destiny, but also your personality, your relationships, and even the way others perceive your presence. In this constant exchange between cosmic and inner energies, numbers merge with letters, resulting in a unique combination that resonates in your name, like a mantra representing you.

Imagine the sound of a bell resonating and expanding in the air. **The letters and numbers in your name act in a similar way**, emitting vibrations that affect how you present yourself to others and how they perceive you. Every word you speak carries with it an energy wave, and every letter and number in your name communicates a part of you, creating a frequency that spreads around you, leaving a trace. It is as if your name is a melody that few can decipher, a note that carries your virtues and secrets, visible only to those who can truly listen.

Each letter of your name has a meaning and a story, and when we link it to a number, that story takes shape. Each number, linked to a planet, imprints an esoteric virtue on the letters, creating patterns and resonances. That is why the name you bear speaks of you. A name is never random; it is an interweaving of forces that you attract and bring into the world.

Think of your name as a door: some may perceive only the facade, but those who can interpret the energies hidden in the letters can open it and discover what lies within. When we speak our name, we evoke the energies of the numbers that represent the letters, giving rise to a current of force that not only influences the way we are perceived, but also accompanies us like a guide, a kind of invisible guardian.

Imagine that you can see each number that makes up your name as an ancient symbol, **a bridge between you and cosmic forces**. Each number, in this esoteric system, carries its virtue, its light and also its shadows. There are no vibrations without nuances, just as there is no light without shadow. Some numbers emanate positive energies, attract abundance and foster spiritual connection; others, when they come into imbalance, can bring challenges and obstacles, teaching you that every force has its dark side.

Perhaps you have noticed how, on some days, you seem to emanate more confidence, and on others you feel uncertain, as if a veil covers your light. This happens because **numbers and letters are not static**: like the stars and planets, they also move and change, reflecting your mood, your desires, your fears. In this way, your name resonates differently each time you say it, depending on the energy you carry within you.

Then there are those numbers that, more than others, have such a powerful influence that they can reveal unexpected aspects, sides of you that you may not even know. The strongest energies, especially those related to the Master Numbers, carry with them responsibilities and require constant balance. Those who possess these intense vibrations know how complex it can be to manage them. A name that contains these numbers has the power to attract great potential, but also to bring to the surface dark sides, forces that, if unrecognized, can manifest in unexpected ways. This is why it is so important to learn about one's vibration. Knowing what energies lie within your name gives you the power to understand your path, to recognize what virtues you awaken and what challenges you may encounter. **Chaldean numerology allows you to see** beyond the **visible**, to go beyond the surface and discover the power you carry within you.

Don't be surprised if, as you learn, you recognize characteristics or traits in yourself that you previously ignored. Perhaps you will discover that you have an unexpected strength, or conversely, a sensitivity that makes you vulnerable in certain situations. But remember that this vulnerability can become your greatest asset, just like a light that shines only on the darkest nights. If there is one lesson Chaldean numerology teaches, it is that **each name is a universe unto itself**, a reflection of the stars, planets, and cosmic energies. Each number imprints an esoteric virtue in the letters, giving you qualities that you can awaken or transform. Each name is an invitation to explore yourself and discover hidden potential, to make visible what is invisible.

And so, your name becomes a bridge between you and the universe, a living connection that speaks to you, guides you, reveals who you really are.

The Chaldean system and the Pythagorean system

Imagine for a moment that your name, that simple sound that defines you, is much more than a combination of letters. Each word, each letter that makes up your name, carries with it a vibration, a trace of energy that affects who you are and how you are perceived. **This is one of the most powerful secrets of** Chaldean **numerology**: through an ancient language of symbols and numbers, the Chaldeans revealed the hidden essence behind every name, word and sound.

But what makes the Chaldean system so special? Unlike the Western numerological system, which is often limited to an ordered sequence of numbers from 1 to 9, Chaldean numerology grew out of a much deeper esoteric understanding. For the Chaldeans, **each number possessed a unique and sacred energy**, influenced by the vibrations of the cosmos, the planets and those celestial forces they believed acted upon us. In the Chaldean system, numbers are not just mathematical symbols; they carry esoteric qualities and astrological virtues that act as true energy codes.

This numerological system is also distinguished by the respect it shows toward the number 9, a number that the Chaldeans considered sacred and mysterious. For them, 9 represented infinity, eternity, since every multiplication of it always rejoins itself. This respect excluded it from the normal numerical table, elevating it to an almost mystical dimension. That is why in the Chaldean system, **the 9 is not found among the numbers used to calculate letters**, and appears only in the totals, like a silent messenger of infinity.

Unlike the Pythagorean system, which places great emphasis on the birth name, Chaldean numerology focuses on the name you currently use, the one that resonates with today's energy, the one that accompanies you in your daily life. The name by which you present yourself, by which you are called, **carries the energy of who you are at this moment**. It is as if this name captures your present vibrations, the forces you are channeling now, the ones that influence you and guide you through the days and nights.

Think about it: every time your name changes, so does the energy around you. Marriage, divorce, nicknames--each name creates a new energetic imprint, like a note added to your personal melody. It is not just a matter of choice or social convention; it is a profound transformation that affects your relationships, your successes and your obstacles. **Each name is a door that opens new paths and possibilities**.

This is a system that is unparalleled in the numerological world. The Chaldean system is unique, profound, mysterious, and has roots that are lost in time. The symbols and numbers we use today are the result of a long journey from cuneiform, the ancient writing of the Chaldeans, which consisted of linear signs impressed on wet clay. The Chaldeans used straight lines not by accident: it was the most effective method of engraving quickly and accurately on still-soft clay tablets, preserving their messages and knowledge for centuries.

This knowledge has spanned time. From cuneiform, it has been passed down through other languages and cultures: from Egyptian hieroglyphics to Greek letters, from Latin inscriptions to the alphabet we know today. But the essence of what the Chaldeans gave us, that wisdom that looks to letters and numbers as tools of transformation, has never changed. It has remained alive, a secret art that we can still explore.

Today, our alphabet is much more than a set of letters. **It is a language that speaks its own language**, and Chaldean numerology has the power to translate what it is telling us. To calculate your numbers with this system is to embark on a journey to yourself, a journey in which every symbol, every digit, and every letter becomes a guide to your most authentic essence. The Chaldean system does not require complex calculations on vowels or consonants; it is based on a deep understanding of each individual letter, allowing you to discover hidden aspects of you.

Chaldean numerology **is not just any oracle**. It is a tool for self-knowledge that reveals how you relate to the world, how your energies resonate with those around you, and how all of this affects your path. With each calculation, with each number, you learn to recognize what is visible about you and what remains hidden. Each symbol invites you to look further, not to stop at the surface, but to explore the depths of your soul.

This system shows you the power hidden in the letters of your name and gives you access to an awareness that can transform the way you live your life. **Your name becomes a reflection of your destiny, a secret key that opens the doors to the unseen**. You begin to understand that words, just like numbers, live, breathe and speak. They carry with them memories and powers, rooted in the centuries and the earth, as if their very existence were linked to the stars and planets.

Chaldean numerology is, therefore, **a sacred journey to your deepest identity**. It is a journey that requires not only intellectual understanding, but also an openness of heart and spirit. When we pronounce a name, the vibrations of each letter carry with them the energy of planetary virtues, transmitting a kind of "cosmic imprint" on the wearer. Sound and symbol merge, and the name becomes the seal that protects and guides the wearer.

Imagine being able to discover the secret meaning of the letters of your name, to see them as little energetic amulets, each with its own power. Each letter holds an intention, a virtue, a quality that enriches your path, and the whole name resonates like a spell that attracts what you need and protects you from what you do not need. **In this way, Chaldean numerology becomes a ritual of connection with the universe**, a way to ground yourself in the present while expanding into the cosmos.

Each name, then, is like an open portal to mystery. The vibrations enclosed in the letters and numbers become a dance of subtle energies, a timeless song that reminds us of who we are and what we are meant to become. There is nothing random about what the Chaldean system reveals. Every sound, every symbol is a fragment of a larger pattern, an invisible weave that connects your path to the whole.

The Chaldean graph

Diving into the calculations of the Chaldean system is like following an ancient path, a road beaten by centuries of mystery and hidden wisdom. Each letter of your name, each digit that makes up your life path, is charged with a unique vibration, a truth just waiting to be revealed. This chapter will take you through the process of discovering and connecting with the numerical essence of your name, the energy you project into the world, and the message each letter is meant to communicate to you.

Start with the name you use most frequently. The Chaldean system considers the current name, the one you use that represents you in the world, as it encapsulates the vibrations that influence your daily life. It does not matter what first name is registered at the registry office; what matters is the active vibration, the one that resonates every time someone calls you or when you yourself introduce yourself to others. Every time we speak a name, we emit a vibration that imprints itself on the surrounding energy. **Chaldean numerology invites you to explore this very active vibration**, for it is the one that reflects your "here and now" and determines how you are perceived and how you interact with the world.

First, you may find it helpful to hand-draw a version of the Chaldean graph that you will use for calculations. Holding this tool in your hands, working with it, will connect you even more to the ancient knowledge you are about to explore. **Each number is a door that opens** to hidden qualities, to potentials waiting to manifest, or to karmic lessons longing to be understood. Don't just see the numbers as static symbols, but see them as living energies, each carrying a particular astrological virtue.

Below you will find the Chaldean conversion table, from which you can draw to associate each letter of your name with its respective number. This is the key that will allow you to decipher the vibrations inherent in your name:

1	2	3	4	5	6	7	8
A	B	G	D	E	U	O	F
Q	R	C	M	H	V	Z	P
Y	K	L	T	N	W		
I		S		X			
J							

Take the time to write down the numbers associated with each letter of your name and calculate the total. Remember: **the numerical value of your name is not just a digit; it is a vibration that holds a message for you**.

It unites the microcosm of your personal essence with the macrocosm, that vast system of planetary energies that the ancient Chaldeans observed in the night sky. Esotericism is based on this very concept: **the forces that act in the cosmos also resonate within you**. Each number in the Chaldean system represents a specific quality, a virtue that is imprinted in the letters and imbues your name with hidden and symbolic meanings.

To work with these numbers is to open your eyes to yourself like never before. Each digit, each combination reveals a fragment of your inner being, a story that only you can decipher.

Numerological calculation becomes a personal journey, a discovery of how every aspect of your personality resonates with the universe.

Don't let it be a simple intellectual practice; let it become an intuitive dance, a way to listen to that inner voice that you may have neglected for too long.

In the Chaldean system, once you have identified the numbers, the next step is to understand their interactions, the harmonies or contrasts they create. These numbers represent departments in your life and reflect both strengths and challenges. Do not fear if you find that a number or combination carries a challenging lesson. Warm vibrations do not judge; they only offer you the chance to see clearly, to embrace every aspect of yourself with love and understanding.

Allow yourself time to reflect on what emerges.

This process is not about immediate answers or prepackaged solutions; it is a journey that invites you to explore the silent messages that have accompanied you throughout your life.

When you look at your numbers, don't forget that each figure is there for a reason, a reason that only you can understand in its entirety. Let the meaning emerge slowly, unhurriedly. Sometimes, a simple association or reflection can open unsuspected doors, revealing connections and paths you never imagined.

Keep track of your results and the insights you receive along the way.

This practice will allow you to see patterns and connections, to notice how each number and letter builds a mosaic, a unique inner map. **The final visual summary will be a valuable key to**

understanding your vibrations, your dynamics, what drives you and what roots you.

As you explore this system, you will realize that every name, every digit, every combination of numbers is part of a secret language that the universe uses to speak to you.

Chaldean numerology is more than an occult science; it is a form of self-knowledge, a means of recognizing the most hidden parts of yourself. Embrace this knowledge with an open heart and let the numbers lead you to the discovery of your true essence.

Analysis of names using the Chaldean system

Imagine sitting in front of a blank sheet of paper, pen in hand and your full name written in block letters. This is an intimate and powerful moment when you are about to discover something mysterious and profound about yourself.

Your name, so familiar and yet so full of secrets, is actually a code. A code that, with the help of Chaldean numerology, can reveal to you your hidden traits, the energies you carry, the challenges you are called to overcome.

Take a large sheet of paper and divide the space between first name, possible middle name and last name. Let them breathe, leave space between them, because each of these elements speaks of a different part of you. Further down, write the month and day of your birth, as they too affect the overall vibration that represents you.

Now, above each letter of your name, write the corresponding number according to the traditional Chaldean table.

Below is an example of a conversion table with the name "John Smith" to help you visualize the process:

Letter Number Name: J-O-H-N S-M-I-T-H

J	1	J (1)
O	7	O (7)
H	5	H (5)
N	5	N (5)
S	3	S (3)
M	4	M (4)
I	1	I (1)
T	4	T (4)
H	5	H (5)

Under each letter, you now have a digit that represents the numerical vibration of that specific letter, and consequently the unique aspect of your personality manifested through that part of your name.

Sum the Numbers for Each Name

The next step is to add up the digits of each name individually. Add up the digits for "John," then move on to "Adam" (or a possible middle name), and finally add up the digits for "Smith." **Each of these totals represents a "secondary number,"** a separate and profound indication of how each part of your name contributes to your overall energy.

If the result is a two-digit number, sum these two digits until it is reduced to a single digit. Repeat the process for each name. Once you get a number for each part of the name, you will discover a unique vibration for each fragment of you. It is like looking at the pieces of a mosaic before you see them joined into a larger picture.

The Total Number of the Name

Now combine all the sums of your names to get a single number: **the Total Name Number**. This number is a reflection of yourself, an amalgamation of the different parts of your identity that, together, represent you completely. The Total Name Number encapsulates your universal "gift," that fundamental energy you brought to this earth.

This number represents your highest potential, the inner resources you can rely on and also the challenges you face in realizing your authentic essence. It is the number that echoes in the universe, representing how you are perceived not only by people but by the higher energies and vibrations around you.

The Meaning of Secondary Numbers

Secondary numbers, those derived from individual names, carry important messages. They may point you to latent qualities, aspects to be developed, or traits to be addressed. **These numbers guide you like beacons, revealing the path** you can choose to take to become a more complete and fulfilling version of yourself.

These numbers help you explore yourself and understand the potential contained in each name. The first name might whisper to you about your creative inclinations, the middle name might tell you about your deep connections, and the last name might hold the secrets of your inner strength and roots.

On this journey of deciphering, don't forget that each number has a vibration linked to the energies of the universe. Just as the stars affect the tides, so too do the numbers carry a magnetic charge that touches the deepest chords of your spirit. **Each sum and each number is not just a calculation, but a symbol of who you are**, and invites you to resonate with the universe in a conscious way.

Every time you review your name and discover a number, stop for a moment. Ask yourself what it means to you, what it evokes, and listen to the thoughts and insights that surface. In this process, you connect to an invisible network of ancient wisdom that guides and supports you.

Write down everything you discover and observe how these discoveries connect to your life. Perhaps you will notice synchronicities, coincidences that seem random but speak on a deep level. **This exercise is an ongoing dialogue with the universe**, a way to get in tune with your most authentic vibration.

Over time, you may find that your Total Name Number gives you new insight into your personal mission. Or, you might find comfort in the qualities that each sub-number represents. This number connection makes you aware of who you are, your potential, and how you can walk in the world as a soul in tune with cosmic forces.

Sample Calculation

To help you visualize better, we report here the sample calculation for the name "John Smith."

1. Type "John Smith" and use the conversion table to assign a number to each letter:

   - J (1), O (7), H (5), N (5) - total: 1+7+5+5 = 18

   - S (3), M (4), I (1), T (4), H (5) - total: 3+4+1+4+5 = 17

2. Reduce the totals to single digits:

   - 18 becomes 1+8 = 9

   - 17 becomes 1+7 = 8

3. Combine the secondary numbers for the Total Name Number:

   - 9 + 8 = 17, which further reduces to 1+7 = 8.

The Total Name Number for "John Smith" is 8.

This number represents the big picture-the vibration you carry in your entire existence. It is the gift the universe has bestowed upon you, and if you choose to connect to this energy, you will be able to align with your highest purpose. **Explore and embrace this number as a guide**: it speaks to you about your soul, the talents you can manifest and the challenges that will transform you.

By following these calculations and reflecting on the numbers that emerge, you are traveling within yourself, deciphering the mysteries you carry with you and opening new doors of awareness and growth.

Advanced calculations

When we approach the advanced calculations of Chaldean numerology, we enter a territory of profound complexity, where each multi-digit number is revealed as a mosaic. Each element of the number-units, tens, hundreds, thousands-becomes a piece that tells a story, and together they create a symbolic image that illuminates parts of you that you may never have explored. This is where **the essence of Chaldean numerology really manifests itself**: the simple numbers, with which you begin the journey, are only the prelude. They are the key to entry, the first breath of an ancient language rooted in time and the cosmos.

Starting with single digits is essential. For those at the beginning of this path, the advice is to focus on the single digit, which carries with it a pure and simple vibration, a direct and immediate energy. The single digit is like a precious stone that shines its own light, easy to contemplate and understand. It is not just a guide, but a true teacher that introduces you to the first resonances of numerology. Yet, for those who feel ready to look deeper, there is an advanced system that goes beyond isolated numerals. This unique, and rarely described elsewhere, method allows you to break down complex numbers to reveal their innermost essence.

Imagine each digit as a musical note, and each numerical position-units, tens, hundreds, thousands-as a tone that varies the intensity of the message. In the advanced Chaldean system, units resonate with the vibration of the **number 1**, representing the pure and individual essence, the original "self." The tens take on the quality of the **number 2**, carrying with them the meaning of duality, relationships and cooperation. The hundreds, under the influence of the **number 3**, are the realm of expansion, expression and creation. Finally, the thousands, associated with the **number 4**, speak of solid foundations, stability and the structures that support everything else.

Each digit placed in these planes is not random: it reflects a unique dynamic, a balance of forces acting on your path. This is why, for example, a number like 2019 can be "read" as 2 of thousands, 0 of hundreds, 1 of tens, and 9 of units. Each of these numbers has its own weight, and together they create a specific vibration, an energy that pulses and lives in resonance with your soul.

But remember, this is not a race against time, and there is no need to rush to calculate and interpret complex numbers or concepts such as the Karmic Path or Life Number. **Each number deserves its own space and time to be understood**, just as each thought and emotion needs to be experienced to reveal its true nature. Delving into advanced numbers requires experience and a solid foundation, an understanding that goes beyond initial curiosity. It is like digging a well: the deeper you go, the more your connection to the underground waters, the hidden depths of your being, intensifies.

The advanced system is available to you for when you are ready, for when your path leads you to want to discover those hidden symbols that only complex numbers can reveal. The numerological path, after all, is a journey of inner growth, and Chaldean numerology invites you to explore these advanced calculations only when you feel truly confident, as if each digit and value has already come to life in your mind and heart. Taking time to savor each discovery will allow you to build an authentic connection with the numbers, making each interpretation one more step in your personal evolution.

And like any path of awareness, numerology finds its beauty in practice. Take the time to practice, experiment with the numbers and the vibrations that emerge from your name and date of birth. Let each digit reveal its meaning slowly, without forcing it. **It is a journey of discovery, and each number has a message for** you-don't be in a hurry to reveal it all at once.

When you are ready to learn more about the secrets of this ancient science, Templum Dianae will be here to accompany you. Stay in touch with us to learn about future publications on Chaldean numerology and esoteric arts. Each stage of this journey is a door that opens to new worlds, and you are the keeper of the keys.

GUİDED EXERCİSES

Imagine plunging into a space suspended in time, a place that exists only for you and your questions. **An enveloping silence** settles around you, like a subtle mist whispering ancient truths. In this space of mystery and contemplation, you feel a call. It is something that draws you in, an energy that vibrates between your heart and mind. A faint signal, like an invisible touch, suggests to you that there are answers -- but not in words. The answers are in the numbers.

Thus begins your journey, a journey that asks you to trust your senses, to sharpen your perception to grasp nuances invisible to the eyes. **Numbers are not just symbols**: they are portals, keys to subtle realities, mysteries that call you to discover what is hidden. The invitation is simple, but profound. I ask you to let go of logical thinking, to surrender to pure sensation, to the subtle energy flowing around you. Take these exercises as a kind of personal ritual, a sacred space where you can meet each figure as a friend, a guide.

Are you ready to dance with the energy of numbers? There is no hurry, no strict rules. **Just sit comfortably** and let your breath find a slow, deep rhythm. Each exhalation brings you a little closer to this inner space, where the numbers come alive. Here are the steps to get started. Don't worry if something doesn't seem clear at first or if your heart doesn't catch every signal right away. This path is personal, intimate, and each encounter with a number is an act of pure trust.

Visualization and meditation.

Close your eyes. Breathe deeply and let the world fade away for a moment, dissolving into silence. You are in a space that you know well, and yet, at the same time, it has a mysterious and secret air, like a hidden room inside you. It is here that every number whispers, that every digit reveals its secret. This is a time dedicated to you, to your connection with the deep and subtle energies. Are you ready to discover what each number can bring to your life?

Start by choosing a number that attracts you, like a musical note that resonates only for you. Observe which number calls to you. It may be one related to your birth date, or one you encounter often, in coincidences, in dreams. Let your instincts guide you. It is not the number that is chosen: it is it that has chosen you, and you respond to its call.

Imagine now that the number takes shape, like a light suspended in the center of your being. **See this clear, vibrant light**. It is more than just a number, it is a living essence. Like a flower slowly opening, let the number show itself in all its energy. Feel its vibration: it is a growing, expanding presence until it becomes clear, almost tangible. Don't be in a hurry. Stay listening, with no need to explain or interpret. The act will make itself understood.

Now close your eyes and bring your attention to the planetary significance of the number. Each number in Chaldean numerology **is linked to a planet**, which infuses its characteristics. If you chose the number two, imagine the energy of the Moon. Perceive it as a cool, deep caress, like a wave that slowly rises, then gently recedes. This is lunar energy: calm, gentle, sometimes mysterious. Let it envelop you. If you have chosen the number five, feel Mercury's quick, unpredictable energy, like a crisp breeze that urges your thoughts to flow and play, lightly. Whatever number you chose, **connect with the planet that represents it**.

Stay in this space, listening. Let the energy of the number make its way into you, without trying to control it. It is a subtle but powerful energy. It is as if the number is speaking to you, but not with words. It is a language made of vibrations, of insights. **Let it reveal itself**. Don't try to understand it right away. There is a time for every revelation, and now is the time to receive, not to analyze.

Each number has a frequency, a unique voice that you can feel. It is as if it is showing you a new language, a language made of energy. Recognizing these vibrations brings you closer to the true essence of each number. It is a connection that needs no logic, only sensitivity. Allow yourself to enter into this dance with the number, without expectations.

Repeat this exercise each day with a different number. Each one has a message, a planetary essence that offers you a way to look at the world and yourself from new perspectives. Observe how the number changes your inner state, how its vibration mixes with yours. It is a process that takes time and patience, but it brings with it **a new awareness**. Through meditation, let the number become a part of you, let it enter your inner world, enriching it.

Over time, you will notice that each issue will begin to reveal hidden aspects of you. It will be like **an inner map** revealing itself bit by bit, made of light, vibration, and knowledge. You will discover how each number is a doorway, a path to be traveled to reach deeper levels of your soul. And as you continue these exercises, your connection with the world of numbers will grow, become stronger, until it becomes part of your daily awareness.

Each number shows you a way into a world of subtle and powerful energies. Your journey with the numbers is never just an exercise: it is a path of inner awakening. **Embrace each number as a teacher**, as an ally who accompanies you toward a greater understanding of who you are.

Finally, be patient with yourself. Chaldean numerology is not an exact science: it is a way, a path that winds in and out of you. It is not about learning formulas or definitions, but about feeling, sensing what the number wants to reveal to you. It is a silent dialogue, a discovery that grows day by day.

The Shadow Book of Numbers.

Now is the time to create a sacred place to keep the secrets that numerology reveals to you. **Imagine a book just yours**, a silent guide, a companion who observes you and collects the signs of your journey. It will be your numbers notebook, a journal that will accompany you whenever you feel the need to gain clarity or dive into the magic of numerological calculations.

Choose a special notebook, one that inspires you and is beautiful just to hold in your hands. This will not be a simple notebook: **it is your Book of Number Shadows**. Each page you write will have meaning, each line will become a small doorway to your inner world. Don't rush, let time guide you and let every calculation, every name written here be a kind of ritual, a gesture of connection with the universe of numbers.

Imagine starting with the basics: write your first name, then your last name, and start calculating its numerological value. Each letter has a number, and each number holds a power. Feel the vibrations as you do the calculations, feel the energy emanating from the numbers. Your name is more than a set of letters: it is a key, a pitch that resonates and aligns with the cosmos.

Continue with the names of people who are important to you. The numbers that emerge will tell you a lot about them and the bond you have. Write down their names carefully, noting the calculations and the feelings that come to you. Don't think of the numbers as static results, but as voices that speak to you of past stories, possible paths, challenges and harmonies. Feel the vibrations that resonate in these connections, like waves that overlap or recede. In time, the pages of this book will become a map for you, a guide for understanding your relationships, for sensing what unites you and what alienates you from others.

Even dates can reveal secrets. Every special moment has its own numerical code: birthdays, anniversaries, important dates in your life or in the lives of people you love. Note them down and calculate their numerological significance. Feel how each date speaks to you of an energy, a cycle, a growing and expanding movement. You may find that some dates repeat, that some numbers return as signals, as little messages the universe sends you. Let your book become a refuge for these signs. There are no rigid rules: follow your instincts and allow yourself to explore.

As you write, let your intuition guide you. Each number, each calculation is a step in your quest, a piece added to the mosaic. **Don't try to figure everything out right away**. The beauty of numerology is its mystery, its ability to reveal itself slowly, one fragment at a time. Each time you go back and read what you have jotted down, you will be different, and the numbers will reveal something new.

This notebook will be your companion, a place to write down even thoughts, insights that arise during your meditations. After each exercise, take a few moments to write down what you felt. If a particular number spoke to you, describe what you sensed, if you felt an emotion, a memory. Let these words guide you over time. It may be that as you reread them one day, you will catch a meaning that you did not initially see.

This Shadow Book of Numbers will be your silent friend, a keeper of the revelations that only you have discovered. In time, you will notice how each digit, each name, each date is a doorway to a hidden part of you, and how each calculation brings you closer to your essence. This book will become **a mirror of your inner journey**, a reference point to better understand what you are experiencing, the energies around you, and the signals the universe is sending you.

As the days go by, whenever you feel confused or in search of answers, you can return to this book, and the pages will speak to you. All you have to do is open it and reread the words you have written to find meaning, direction, meaning. There is no need to analyze everything, nor to look for logical explanations. Numbers speak a language that reveals itself slowly, requiring patience and listening.

Through this notebook, you are making a deep connection with the forces that guide your path. Every time you write, every time you add a name or a date, you are cultivating an intimate dialogue with the mystery of numbers. **This is your map, your guide**, a path that reveals itself a little at a time, and becomes clearer as you travel it.

And so, page after page, calculation after calculation, you will begin to see how everything is connected. You will recognize the patterns, the repetitions, the signals that emerge through the figures. This book will help you chart a path of awareness, like a golden thread guiding you through the labyrinth of your questions and answers.

Eventually, your Numbers Book of Shadows will be a precious refuge, a space where time stands still and truths are gently revealed. It will not be just a notebook: it will become **an extension of your soul**, a place that accompanies you on your spiritual journey. Each time you open it, you will feel that you are returning home, to the center of yourself.

Rituals with herbs and crystals.

Now is the time to connect to each number not only through thought, but **through the tangible energy** of the herbs and crystals, linked to the planets that rule these numbers. Each number carries with it an ancient and powerful vibration, and you can call it up here, now, through a small ritual.

Begin by choosing the number you wish to work with. Feel the energy of that number as a living presence, an invisible essence waiting to reveal itself. **Each number is linked to a planet**, and each planet has stones and plants that amplify its energy. If you are working, for example, with the number six, you will feel the call of Venus. Take rose quartz and a few dried rose petals. **Light a candle** and let the energy of the quartz and the delicate scent of the rose fill the room.

Take a moment to contemplate the stone, feel its cool surface under your fingers, observe its soft light. As you close your eyes, imagine the number six shining before you, wrapped in an aura of light and love. Breathe deeply and let the energy of Venus envelop you, like a mantle of tenderness and peace.

This ritual is simple, but powerful. **You don't need rare or hard-to-find items**: often the herbs are ones you already have in your kitchen or garden, and even a small crystal can hold great energy, as long as it is authentic. The key is intention, a willingness to create a sacred space and connect deeply with the number you have chosen. You can repeat this ritual with different numbers, discovering how each one has a voice, a unique vibration, that speaks to you in a different way.

Place the stone and grass dedicated to that number in front of you and allow yourself to be transported. Close your eyes and imagine the number shining, surrounded by the aura of its planetary essence. Each number is a portal to a hidden world, and as you focus on it, feel how it strengthens, how its energy resonates with you, how it becomes part of you.

Stay open to what you perceive. Perhaps you will feel a sensation in your body, or a sudden intuition. An image may appear in your mind, or an unexpected emotion. **This is the subtle language of numbers and planets**, a language that is spoken not with words but with vibrations, with symbols, with small signals that only the heart can decipher. Every exercise, every ritual you practice is a step toward deeper awareness, a way to root in you the connection with the numbers. Every time you sit and contemplate a number, you feel how numerology becomes part of you, how it becomes a way to see the world and to understand even your most intimate experiences. It is a journey that requires patience, but one that brings with it **great wisdom**, ancient knowledge that accompanies you along the way.

Here is a simple table of associations to help you choose the right stone and herb for each issue:

Number	Planet	Crystal	Grass
1	Sunshine	Tiger eye	Laurel
2	Moon	Moonstone	Chamomile
3	Jupiter	Amethyst	Sage
4	Uranus	Aquamarine	Rosemary
5	Mercury	Green quartz	Lavender
6	Venus	Rose quartz	Pink
7	Neptune	Amethyst	Jasmine
8	Saturn	Onyx	Myrrh
9	Mars	Carnelian	Thyme

Use this chart as a guide, but be inspired by your intuition. Feel which stone or herb is calling to you in a particular way, which vibration resonates with your energy at this moment. There are no hard rules: these are tools, portals that help you get in touch with the invisible world of numbers.

Whenever you perform a ritual, remember to let go of any hurry, to give time to time. Each number has its own wisdom to reveal, and sometimes it takes patience. Even just lighting a candle and contemplating the flame, with the crystal in your hands and the grass scenting the air, is already a way to open a dialogue with the universe. **The mystery of numbers is not revealed all at**

once: it is a journey, a journey that transforms you, bringing you closer to your true essence.

Let yourself be guided by the pleasure of discovering each number as if it were an encounter, an intimate dialogue with the energy of the cosmos. In time, you will feel that numerology becomes a second skin, a way to observe not only the outer world, but also your inner world. Each number is like a star shining in your personal constellation, and you are learning about its position, influence, and meaning.

Finally, keep this ritual as a small refuge to return to whenever you feel the need for guidance, a sign, or advice. And when you are ready to unravel new mysteries, keep in touch with **Templum Dianae**. With upcoming publications, we will continue to explore the secrets of Chaldean numerology and esoteric arts together, opening new doors on the journey toward self-knowledge and self-discovery.

CONCLUSION

We have come to the end of this journey, but the path of Chaldean numerology is much broader than you might imagine. Each page of this book has brought you a little closer to ancient wisdom, to those secret keys that reside at the heart of each number, ready to reveal themselves only to those who have the patience to seek. But know, dear soul on the way, that **one reading is not enough**. Chaldean numerology is like a labyrinth of mirrors: each time you return to these concepts, you discover new reflections, different perspectives, deeper levels of understanding. This book is not a manual to flip through and put away; it is a living work, evolving with you.

Take the time to immerse yourself again and again in his words. **Each rereading is a deeper step** into your connection with the numbers and your subconscious. Repetition, in this journey, is not just study, but a way to open hidden doors. Know that the numbers and their esoteric vibrations also have the ability to affect you in subtle ways, acting at the soul level and igniting insights, cues, and memories that emerge from deep within. **Reread this text at least five times.** Yes, you got it right: five times. Only in this way will the occult keys be able to activate, awakening that latent knowledge that is already within you. You are not here to accumulate knowledge, but to awaken what you already know. The power of Chaldean numerology goes beyond the rational mind; it enters the domain of mystery, the sphere of perceptions and intuitions that speak to your subconscious. Each number carries a secret message, and each word you read is a spark that, repeated over time, awakens your inner power.

Each time you reread, a new layer reveals itself. Words will seem to change, concepts to take a different shape, as if **Chaldean numerology has its own consciousness**, ready to give you answers only when you are really ready to receive them. Don't be in a hurry, don't try to understand everything right away. Let the magic of repetition work for you, allowing each symbol, each calculation, to dig deep and touch chords you didn't even know you had. Imagine this process as a ritual. Each rereading is a small initiation, a call that the universe sends you to remind you of who you are, to show you new nuances of your path. Don't just read with your mind, but with your heart, with your intuition. Feel how each word envelops you, like a thin cloak that fits over your skin, awakening ancient knowledge. And as you reread, you will feel that the book itself speaks to you, that each sentence carries an echo, an energy that is amplified. But don't stop there. This is just the beginning of a journey. **Templum Dianae will continue to explore the secrets of Chaldean numerology** and esoteric arts, opening doors to deeper knowledge, to mysteries yet unexplored. Each publication will be a new fragment of this journey, another step in your discovery of the truth that resides in the universe of numbers. We invite you to follow us, to let us guide you in this never-ending exploration. Each text will be a new key, a new way of understanding and deepening your connection with occult knowledge.

Think of this book as a map, but a map that is enriched and transformed every time you return to it. **Each reading creates a wave that activates your subconscious**. It is a path made of cycles, and each cycle brings you closer to your essence, to that part of you that has always known what the numbers, the vibrations, the symbols really mean. Chaldean numerology is not an exact science, but an ancient art, a subtle dance between you and the unseen world. And that takes time, dedication, openness.

Rereading the manual means not only understanding it better, but **allowing its words to become part of you**. The more you practice, the more you feel that this knowledge becomes intertwined with your life, that it takes root deep inside you. Each page becomes a reflection of your path, each issue a silent guide, a lantern illuminating your steps. And in time, without almost noticing it, you will feel the Chaldean numerology flowing through you like a river, fluid and natural, effortless.

This is not a conclusion, dear soul. It is only a passing point, a call to continue, to dive in again and again, like an explorer discovering new worlds. Be curious, be patient. Secrets are revealed to those who know how to listen, to those who know how to wait. You don't need anything but trust. **Every time you reread, you activate a new part of yourself**, like a light that gradually comes on. There is nothing final in this journey: the real magic is hidden in the going forward, in the discovery that never ends. So, when you feel the call, return to these pages. Let the words work on you, take you once again through the symbols, the vibrations, the energies. With each reread, you will discover new depths, and effortlessly, Chaldean numerology will become a faithful guide, a key to reading not only the world around you, but also the world within you.

When you are ready for new mysteries, remember that Templum Dianae will be there to accompany you. There is still much to explore, and we will guide you along the paths less traveled, to **the answers you seek**. We are here on this journey together, and the future still holds many secrets.

Conclusion

GLOSSARY OF TERMS

☐ **Numerology**: Study of the esoteric meaning of numbers and their impact on human events.

☐ **Digit**: A single number.

☐ **Destiny Number**: A number derived from the date of birth that indicates major challenges and life lessons.

☐ **Soul Number**: Number representing a person's inner desires and motivations.

☐ **Number of Expression**: Number describing natural potentials and talents.

☐ **Birth** Number: Direct number of the day of birth that has its own influences.

☐ **Life Path**: A number calculated from the date of birth that shows the main direction of a person's life.

☐ **Personal Year**: Number indicating trends and outlook for a specific year.

☐ **Personal Month**: Number describing the energies for a particular month.

☐ **Personal Day**: Number that affects daily activities.

☐ **Master Numbers**: Numbers composed of duplicate digits (such as 11, 22, 33) that carry greater potential.

☐ **Numerological** Kabbalah: Application of numerology based on Kabbalistic principles.

☐ **Chaldean** Numerology: A numerological system that assigns numerical values to letters based on their vibration.

☐ **Pythagorean Numerology**: A system that assigns numerical values to letters based on their position in the alphabet.

☐ **Root** Number: The base number of a number after it has been reduced (adding the digits together to make a single number).

☐ **Cyclic** Number: A number that indicates repeated periods of time in a person's life.

☐ **Pythagorean** Table: Table used to convert letters to numbers in Pythagorean numerology.

☐ **Arc of Transformation**: Interval of years in which a person experiences significant changes.

☐ **Karmic** Numbers: Numbers indicating karmic lessons to be learned in this life.

☐ **Angel Numbers**: Number sequences believed to be messages from angels.

☐ **Numerical Synergy**: The energetic interaction between different numbers.

☐ **Challenge Numbers**: Numbers representing personal obstacles to overcome.

☐ **Numbers of Opportunity**: Numbers that indicate potential moments of luck or success.

☐ **Repetitive Numbers**: Sequences of numbers that appear repeatedly in a person's life.

☐ **Numerology Matrix**: Complete pattern of a person's numbers derived from his or her date of birth and full name.

☐ **Astro-Numerology**: The integration of numerology with astrology.

☐ **Solar Numbers**: Numbers associated with the Sun that influence the outward personality.

☐ **Lunar** Numbers: Moon-related numbers that influence emotions and intuition.

☐ **Reality Numbers**: Numbers that represent a person's external perception.

☐ **Harmonization Framework**: A numerical configuration showing how to balance personal energies.

☐ **Dynamic** Numbers: Numbers that indicate movement and change in a person's life.

☐ **Static Numbers**: Numbers indicating stability and persistence.

☐ **Balancing Numbers**: Numbers that help balance other numerical energies.

☐ **Transitory Analysis**: Study of the numbers that affect a person during a specific period.

☐ **Evolutionary Numbers**: Numbers representing personal growth and development through life.

☐ **Compatibility Number**: Number indicating numerological compatibility between two people.

☐ **Conflict** Number: Number indicating potential challenges in relationships.

☐ **Number of Synthesis**: Number representing the integration of different energies.

☐ **Potential Number**: Number indicating future possibilities.

☐ **Resonance** Number: Number that resonates most strongly with a person or situation.

☐ **Numerical Code**: A specific set of numbers that have special meaning for a person.

☐ **Activation** Number: Number that activates or triggers specific events or energies.

☐ **Subtle** Numbers: Numbers that influence in less obvious or direct ways.

☐ **Growth Numbers**: Numbers indicating areas of potential expansion.

☐ **Resonance** Number: Number that has special resonance or importance.

☐ **Transition** Numbers: Numbers that signal changes or transitions.

☐ **Elemental Numbers**: Numbers associated with the classical elements (earth, air, fire, water).

☐ **Foundation Numbers**: Numbers that form the basis of a personality or situation.

☐ **Culmination** Numbers: Numbers that represent the achievement of a goal or understanding.

☐ **Universal** Numbers: Numbers that have a general and globally applicable meaning.

☐ **Personal Numbers**: Numbers that have specific meaning for the individual.

☐ **Turning** Point Numbers: Numbers that indicate times of great change or decision.

☐ **Mystical** Numbers: Numbers that carry with them a deeply spiritual or mysterious meaning.

☐ **Balance** Number: Number that helps maintain or restore energy balance.

☐ **Energy Numbers**: Numbers that represent different forms of energy in a person's life.

☐ **Revelation** Number: Number that reveals hidden or non-manifest information.

☐ **Numbers of Intensity**: Numbers that intensify energies or experiences.

☐ **Number of Reconciliation**: Number that helps resolve conflicts or differences.

☐ **Ascension Numbers**: Numbers representing spiritual elevation or development.

☐ **Start Number**: Number that signals the beginning of a new cycle or phase.

☐ **Closure Number**: Number indicating termination or completion.

☐ **Fixation Numbers**: Numbers that stabilize a situation or condition.

☐ **Major Challenge Numbers**: Numbers that represent significant challenges that need to be addressed.

☐ **Support** Numbers: Numbers that offer support or assistance.

☐ **Protection** Numbers: Numbers that provide protection or defense.

☐ **Liberation** Numbers: Numbers that facilitate liberation from constraints or restrictions.

☐ **Restoration** Numbers: Numbers that help restore conditions or situations.

☐ Numbers **of Transformation**: Numbers that indicate or facilitate profound change.

☐ **Purification** Numbers: Numbers that help clarify or purify situations.

☐ **Numbers of Enlightenment**: Numbers that bring clarity, understanding or enlightenment.

☐ **Manifestation** Numbers: Numbers that help manifest desires or intentions.

☐ **Strengthening** Numbers: Numbers that increase strength or endurance

Glossary of terms

ANOTHER BOOK FROM TEMPLUM DIANAE FOR YOU

https://www.amazon.com/Dark-Goddesses-Morrigan-exercises-meditations/dp/B0DJS4N3Z4

the book of testimony

What women readers are saying about Templum Dianae Books. (in all languages)

 Marruskaa

★★★★★ **Bella scoperta**
Recensito in Italia il 12 agosto 2024

Il testo è scritto in modo chiaro e scorrevole, perfetto per principianti! Quando mi sono avvicinata a questo tipo di mondo all'inizio non avevo ben capito cosa fossero e a cosa servissero. Tuttavia, il loro fascino mi ha spinto a continuare cercare di capire, finché non ho trovato questo libro. Ora tengo questo tomo sempre sul mio comodino e non posso più farne a meno! Davvero consigliato!

 Jamie L.

★★★★★ **Learn about powerful archetypes and how to use them for yourself!**
Reviewed in the United States on October 12, 2024
Verified Purchase

This book gives a comprehensive overview of dark goddesses from different times and regions-- Egyptian, Slavic, Roman, Greek, etc.

It gives enough information about each that you can feel into which one speaks to you at different times in your life.

I've often heard people talk about "working with" goddesses or goddess energies and I had no idea what that meant or how to do it! This book provides different ways to do this--like specific rituals or practices (and there's even a guided meditation with a link to an MP3 file included!) so you can not only learn about the goddesses but also start to incorporate different practices to begin working with them for your own personal transformation.

 Rose Anderson

★★★★★ **Beautifully written and immensely powerful**
Reviewed in the United States on October 8, 2024
Verified Purchase

What a wonderful gift for any modern-day witch or pagan—and everyone else, too.

The first part of "Wicca Lunar Calendar—2025" offers insight for living in these times, self-care, and even wisdom of the cosmos—for a start. It then goes through every month of 2025 in almanac style, with the cycles of the moon, the holidays, and more. There's also a glossary at the end.

It's beautifully written and immensely powerful.

 dorawatson96

★★★★★ **nützlich für diejenigen, die sich Wicca nähern**

Bewertet in Deutschland am 1. Oktober 2024

Ich habe mich dieser Welt im letzten Jahr genähert und habe diesen Kalender in meiner Bibliothek. Ich finde ihn sehr nützlich als Unterstützung auf diesem Weg, den ich eingeschlagen habe

 Narnya

★★★★★ **Sehr interessant**

Bewertet in Deutschland am 12. Oktober 2024

Verifizierter Kauf

Endlich eine gute Beschreibung über Samhain. Zur Erinnerung. Ich werde das Buch weiter meinen Kindern auch empfehlen. Vielle Dank ☆

 Geneviève

★★★★★ **Très intéressant**

Avis laissé au Canada le 1 mars 2024

Achat vérifié

Grand calendrier lunaire, très complet et beaucoup d'explications intéressantes. Parfait pour associer au livre de wicca magie blanche.

 Steven H.

★★★★★ **Una Guía Completa de la Numerología Antigua y los Números Angelicales**

Reviewed in the United States on August 1, 2024

"La Numerología degli Antichi - Numerología Caldea e Numeri Angelici" es una compilación excepcional para cualquiera fascinado por el mundo místico de los números. Este paquete 3 en 1 cubre los detalles intrincados de la numerología, el significado de los números angelicales y los sistemas de numerología antigua, ofreciendo una exploración completa y atractiva de estos temas.

El autor proporciona tablas, cálculos y explicaciones claras y detalladas, haciendo que los conceptos complejos sean accesibles tanto para principiantes como para entusiastas experimentados de la numerología. Cada sección está bien estructurada, permitiendo a los lectores seguir fácilmente y aplicar el conocimiento a sus propias vidas.

 Ana J

★★★★★ **La Influencia de la Luna**

Reseñado en Estados Unidos el 8 de septiembre de 2024

Compra verificada

Este libro trata de las fases de la luna a la vida moderna, cubriendo todo, desde las rutinas de belleza hasta la jardinería. Al crecer, a menudo escuchaba a los mayores hablar sobre cómo la luna influía en la agricultura y los animales, y este libro refleja esas tradiciones. Las secciones de las fases lunares ofrecen informacion sobre cómo aprovechar la energía lunar para tener resultados óptimos en la jardinería y de belleza. Es una guia interesante para quienes buscan alinear muchas de sus rutinas con la naturaleza.

Another book from
Templum Dianae for you

 Sarah Barry

★★★★☆ **Practical exercises**

Reviewed in the United States on September 30, 2024

Verified Purchase

"Twin Flames: Love Yourself and Manifest Ultimate Love" provides practical exercises for healing emotional blocks and attracting love through the Law of Attraction. Worth reading for those seeking self-love and deeper connections.

 Daphne H

★★★★☆ **Muy bueno!**

Reseñado en Australia el 15 de septiembre de 2024

Compra verificada

Cuidar el jardín a través de los movimientos de la luna es una idea genial, ya que en la naturaleza todo está conectado y sin duda los ciclos lunares pueden influir tanto positiva como negativamente. El libro incluye un montón de tips de los cuáles tomé nota.

 Regina Stone

★★★★☆ **Always been curious...**

Recensito negli Stati Uniti il 28 settembre 2024

Acquisto verificato

I'll be honest: I'm not sure I am the intended audience for this book.

I've never been a firm believer in astrology, but my lifelong curiosity drew me to "Moon Calendar 2025."
It was a fascinating read overall, very interesting even if not 100% convincing to my cynical nature.

I would have given it 5 stars but I did find the book a little too sophisticated a launching point for readers new to astrology. However, if this is not an introduction for you - and you are a believer - then I think you will find value in these pages.

contents included

Congratulations on receiving this book!
If you want to attract and manifest more Love and Abundance
and discover topics and spirituality, join the Templum Dianae
community and receive guided meditation MP3s to awaken
your inner self.

This guided meditation is designed to manifest your inner
dream in daily life.

Follow this link
templumdianae.com/en/bookmp3/

Bibliographical references
and recommended readings

- **Evolutionary Esoteric Numerology** - Templum Dianae Media - 2023
- **The Numbers of Angels** - Templum Dianae Media - 2023